My dear friend & sister, Kristine. You have been so important, showing me His men [are] happening here and [?] You and Frank are God's gift to I know God has some wonderful missions" ahead.

Love, Susan Richardson October, 2022

ENDORSEMENTS

Tony Suarez brings a much-needed word for the hour. Even the book title, *RevivalMakers*, is a bold call for the body of Christ to stop waiting around for a move of God, and start moving—because if God lives inside of you and you move, then you are a move of God. Every word is packed with the bold reminder that if you are born again and filled with the Holy Spirit, you are the solution that, often, you are crying out for and waiting around for.

JENTEZEN FRANKLIN
Senior Pastor, Free Chapel
New York Times bestselling author

Could it be you are waiting on God to do something He has already done? What if the great revival you have been praying for isn't coming but is already here? In Tony's new book, *RevivalMakers*, you will be challenged and inspired to no longer seek revival but rather step into purpose and be a RevivalMaker.

PAULA WHITE CAIN
Pastor, City of Destiny

RevivalMakers is a masterfully written book on revival from a pure Pentecostal perspective from someone we know to carry that mantle deep within his spiritual DNA. Tony clearly articulates what it means and what it takes to be a RevivalMaker. Birthing and hosting revival personally or corporately requires intentionality. This book will lead you down that narrow but glorious path. Tony has left no stone unturned in teaching you how to pay the price. Use these valuable principles and start living the life of a RevivalMaker!

PAUL AND KIM OWENS, Revivalists
Author, *Doorkeepers of Revival*
Pastors, Fresh Start Church
Peoria, Arizona

While some are looking for revival, Tony Suarez is already living in one. If you are seeking to fan the flame of revival in your heart or feel as if revival fire in your heart has been dampened by the chilling chaos of a culture cold toward God, this book is for you. My calling with Pastor Joel Osteen and Lakewood Church is to connect the millions of mostly unbelievers/unchurched people we touch to Bible-based churches! Revival churches that preach hope in Christ and are true *RevivalMakers!* With similar roots and a passion to bear lasting fruit for the Kingdom, we stand wholeheartedly and believe in the crucial and Christ-centered revival message Tony preaches with such godly articulation and anointing.

PHIL MUNSEY
Chairman of Lakewood Church/Joel
Osteen's Champions Network
Houston, Texas

The name Tony Suarez is synonymous with revival— real, life-altering revival. In my opinion Tony's revival conviction makes him one of the most relevant voices speaking today. He has often been called upon by the Church of God denomination to inspire and instruct our pastors in their quest for an authentic move of the Holy Spirit in their local churches. I urge everyone hungry for God to obtain and read a book that matters—*RevivalMakers!*

BISHOP TIM HILL

General Overseer, Church of God

RevivalMakers is that right-now word that will charge and commission you to be the move of God that your family, city, and region are longing for. So get ready—this book is not for the faint of heart. But it is absolutely essential reading for those who want to see the power of God demonstrated today as it was in the Book of Acts. It's mandatory for the radical remnant God is raising up who are tired of complacency, done with gimmicks, and are ready to see nations in revival. The revival you long to see begins with you, for you are a RevivalMaker!

TONY STEWART

Senior Pastor, Citylife Church

Tampa, Florida

My friend Tony Suarez has a heart to see the church experience a move of God that is not just seasonal but perpetual. In his newest book, *RevivalMakers,* he effectively challenges our approach to faith and our relationship with the Holy Spirit. Revival is exactly what our world needs, and it is here! I can tell you personally, it's not just words on a page, but it is his heart and we have experienced it firsthand at Motor City Church. This book is a must-read for anyone desiring a move of God.

Dr. Dave Martin
Speaker and bestselling author
Detroit, Michigan

When a person thinks of RevivalMakers, there are many names that come to mind—Jimmy Swaggart, Oral Roberts, William J. Seymour, Aimee Semple-McPherson, A.A. Allen, and many others. I believe that we can add to that list a modern-day revivalist, one who is full of Pentecostal fire and a God-given ability to see the miraculous—Tony Suarez. Tony has a heart for revival. He has seen revival firsthand throughout this nation and other parts of the world. If you have ever attended one of his meetings, then you know what I'm saying is true. If you haven't yet been to one of his meetings, do whatever you can to attend. Through this book, you will get a taste of what revival is, and you will start believing for your own revival. As Tony states, it will become obvious to all who pick up this book that God is not looking for revival chasers, but *RevivalMakers*!

Gabriel Swaggart
Family Worship Center
Baton Rouge, Louisiana

Tony Suarez is one of the greatest evangelists of our time. He truly is anointed to sound the trumpet of revival and raise a remnant of fire-baptized believers to take the world by storm. Nations are shaking right now, but there is a solution! Creation is groaning, but there is a remedy. A world in turmoil is longing for the appearance of a company of people who recognize "Christ in me" and actually live like the Spirit of the resurrected Jesus lives within them. This is what heals the sick, delivers the oppressed, and even raises the dead—a people who recognize that it's the Spirit of God in them, available to move in power right now.

JONATHAN MILLER
Pastor, New Beginnings Church
Orlando, Florida

RevivalMakers is that right-now word that will charge and commission you to be the move of God that your family, city and region are longing for. So get ready: this book is not for the faint of heart. But it is absolutely essential reading for those who want to see the power of God demonstrated today, as it was in the Book of Acts. It's mandatory for the radical remnant God is raising up who are tired of complacency, done with gimmicks, and are ready to see nations in revival. The revival you long to see begins with you—for you are a RevivalMaker!

KEVIN WALLACE
Pastor, Redemption for the Nations
Chattanooga, Tennessee

RevivalMakers! Rather than chasing after the latest moves of God, why not cause revival to happen where we are? That's the thesis for Tony's new book. It is an impassioned plea from a true revivalist for God's people to stop expecting systems, governments, leaders, or anyone else to bring social transformation, but to begin to change it ourselves. If we will but stir up the gift that is in us, Tony contends that we have the power to change the world right now. After all, we are the Church. And you know what? I agree with him!

DR. R. HEARD
Bishop, Inspire Church
Houston, Texas

I'm just finished reading Tony Suarez's latest book, RevivalMakers, and my spirit is soaring in expectation! Having had a front-row seat to Tony's maturation in ministry, I've seen firsthand how insistent he is that the Church experience the fullness of revival. Tony is filled and full and is an ambassador for an anointing that is both "of old" and brand-new fresh. Follow the steps he is walking in this book and you will be a RevivalMaker, too!

DARRYL W. HOOPER
Senior Pastor, The Church Covington
Covington, Georgia

There has never been a greater time in history for the greatest move of God. In his book RevivalMakers, Tony Suarez gives a powerful clarion call to the Church to passionately burn for everything God is supernaturally doing in the earth. Revival is now!

Jamie Tuttle
Pastor, Dwelling Place Church
Cleveland, Tennessee

At a time when the church has been tested and tried, RevivalMakers will encourage and remind you that the gates of hell cannot prevail against God's church. If you are wondering when the revival we have prayed and worked for is coming, this book will inspire you to believe revival is not coming—revival is here! God has called and commissioned every believer to be a RevivalMaker. Via Tony's new book you will be inspired and challenged to fulfill your calling!

DARRYL STRAWBERRY
New York Times bestselling author

Tony Suarez has meticulously woven family history, past revivals, and modern moves of the Holy Spirit into a beautiful, inspirational tapestry titled RevivalMakers. I am elated over Tony's embrace of the fivefold ministry; he personally is witnessing the very miracles of which he has written. This book is reader friendly and offers unmistakable directions to the "latter house."

MORTON BUSTARD
Morton Bustard Ministries
Alexandria, Louisiana

Darkness has risen and gross darkness has been seen among the cultures in which we live. However, the glory of the Lord is among us now as a spiritual revolution that is arising! In his anointed new book, RevivalMakers, Tony Suarez brilliantly and prophetically shows us that revival is not only already here but that corporately and individually we are the move of God that is happening in this hour. It is a revolution of light, a purposeful overthrow of this darkness through the power of the Holy Ghost. This book is a must for every person who has prayed, desired, hungered, and waited for the glory of God. No more waiting—you have been chosen to be a RevivalMaker to demonstrate His power throughout the earth. Discover how to be powerfully used of God and carry His presence everywhere you go.

HANK and BRENDA KUNNEMAN
Pastors, Lord of Hosts Church and
One Voice Ministries
Omaha, Nebraska

This book is a fresh wind of "ole time religion" imperative for the future of the church. In an extended age of conferences, summits, and symposia, Rev. Tony Suarez reminds us of the enduring need for revival. Importantly, he emphasizes that revival is not merely an event. With Scripture, personal testimony, and spiritual insight, Suarez posits that revival begins in the life, worship, and service of the faithful. This message is "a fierce urgency of now" for the sake of society and in preparation for the life to come.

ANTIPAS L. HARRIS, PhD
President, The Urban Renewal Center
Norfolk, Virginia

RevivalMakers by Tony Suarez sounds the alarm to every true believer to arise and answer the higher calling of this hour—to be filled to overflowing in Holy Spirit power and to transform the world! His mission to enable and activate the body of Christ will liberate the reader from dead religion, political correctness, and the prevailing deceptions of this age. Let this message challenge, inspire, and encourage you to shake off the limitations of the past. Our heavenly Commander and Chief is summoning His mighty army of world-changers in this critical hour. It's time to arise and report for duty!

ANNE GIMENEZ
Bishop, Rock Church International
Virginia Beach, Virginia

Tony Suarez's book *RevivalMakers* is filled with the zeal, the fire, and the truth of what makes for revival! May it help ignite the fire of the Pentecostal experience in every house of worship, every family dwelling, and to the ends of the earth!

THETUS TENNEY
Alexandria, Louisiana

REVIVAL
MAKERS

REVIVAL MAKERS

STOP CHASING A MOVE OF GOD... AND BE ONE!

TONY SUAREZ

DEDICATION

This book is dedicated to the greatest revivalmaker I know, my mother, Anne Suarez.

She is the glue that holds our family together. Any time my father was honored for something he accomplished on earth, he'd always say "... it's because I married Anne."

I can tell you that whatever good has come or will come from my life will be because of God and the incredible mother He blessed our family with.

From baseball games to piano recitals, no one cheered for their son louder than my mom. In the prayer room, no one prayed more intensely for their kids than my mom.

She taught me how to pray, how to study and how to prepare sermons. To this day she's still my first phone call when I need prayer.

Many call her pastor or their mother in the faith, I have the high honor of saying, "that's my mom."

DESTINY IMAGE® PUBLISHERS, INC.

Promoting Inspired Lives."

This book and all other Destiny Image and Destiny Image Fiction books are available at Christian bookstores and distributors worldwide.

For more information on foreign distributors, call 717-532-3040.

Reach us on the Internet: www.destinyimage.com.

ISBN 13 TP: 978-0-7684-6222-7
ISBN 13 eBook: 978-0-7684-6223-4
ISBN 13 HC: 978-0-7684-6225-8
ISBN 13 LP: 978-0-7684-6224-1

For Worldwide Distribution.
1 2 3 4 5 6 7 8 / 26 25 24 23 22

Contents

FOREWORD

God is in the here and now. He is the same yesterday, today, and forever. In Tony Suarez' passionate and prophetic pages that follow, readers will see God's work throughout the centuries and how God's miracle-working power is applicable to our everyday lives today.

We live in a time when digital screens broadcast world events in real time—wars, pandemics, economic chaos. Often the barrage of nonstop negative news overwhelms us. We can begin to wish for a return to simpler times. But "simpler times" are mental myths. Wars, diseases, and economic collapses have occurred throughout history.

The mental myth to wish for "old times" can become a mental trap. Moses saw the glory of God and his face shone so brightly, he had to put on a veil. But later, he veiled his face so the Israelites would not see that the glory had faded (see 2 Cor. 3:13).

When we wish we were in the times of Smith Wigglesworth and Amee Semple McPherson, when we are dreaming about—or faking—those glory days, the mental trap becomes mental madness. Bruce Springsteen captured this in his classic song, "Glory Days." "Trying to recapture a little of the glory," one lyric states, "leaves you with nothing."

The Apostle Paul exposed this very issue in his letter to the Corinthians which reads in full, *"**We are not** like Moses, who used to put a veil over his face so that the Israelites would not gaze at the end of the glory which was fading away"* (2 Cor. 3:13 AMP, emphasis added).

Why would any Christian want to live in the past, when God is right here, right now, wielding his miracle-working power on behalf of those who love and serve him?

A popular saying from the "glory years" of the Pentecostal revival was, "I was born in the fire and can't stand to live in the smoke."

If people who were in that revival couldn't stand to live in merely smoke, how much more should we avoid living in it?

Peter wanted to build three tabernacles on the Mount of Transfiguration. The Lord said, "No!" because you cannot put God's glory in a box. It resides in tabernacles made without hands. It resides in us.

Sure, we can be like people who chase down moves of God in some church or city or crusade. Or, we can be like those who cause revival to break out wherever we go.

We can live off the stories of miracles from years gone by. Or we can live in the miraculous days prophesied by Joel who wrote, *"And it shall come to pass afterward, that I will pour out my spirit upon all flesh"* (Joel 2:28).

We can sit in armchairs and watch old videos of favorite sermons, or we can get on our knees, take God at His Word, and see the greatest move of God in the history of the world.

The Apostle Paul challenges us to be those who *"with unveiled face, beholding as in a mirror the glory of the Lord, are being transformed into the same image from glory to glory, just as from the Lord, the Spirit"* (2 Cor. 3:18 New American Standard Bible).

Peter wrote that we have been born anew into an inheritance incorruptible and undefiled, that does not fade away (see 1 Pet. 1:4).

Why live in the past when God's glory is today? Let's live in revival. Let's take it everywhere we go. Let this powerful book by Tony Suarez spur you to experience more of God's greatness in your life than you ever thought possible.

Rev. Samuel Rodriguez
Lead Pastor, New Season Church
President/CEO, National Hispanic
Christian Leadership Conference
Best-selling Author
Movie Producer

INTRODUCTION

by Rod Parsley

The reason many in the body of Christ are so uncomfortable with the term revival is that they are so unfamiliar with it. Some have most certainly never witnessed a genuine, God-ordained, Holy Spirit-fueled, culture-transforming revival in our country. No wonder the body of Christ here in America doesn't know what it looks like or how to recognize it when it comes.

I need to define what I mean by revival. A revival is when the church, the body of Christ, the band of born-again believers, gets right. Repentance is the language of revival and is, in fact, the essential ingredient because revival begins at the house of God. In order for something to be re-vived, it must first be -vived, if you will. Revival is a necessary precursor to a culture-shaking awakening that changes the moral climate of our cities and the impact is felt like shock waves across the social spectrum of a region, a nation, or the world.

My friend, Pastor Tony Suarez, is no stranger to revival. He has lived in it, breathed it, demonstrated it, prayed for it, and experienced it all his life. He knows what it looks like and what it can do. He also knows when it is not present and how far much of the church has declined as a result of not hungering and thirsting for it. He understands that revival is not supposed to be an event or an activity as much as it is a lifestyle and an everyday outcome of the Holy Spirit operating in and through His people.

For far too long, far too many have been content with church as usual. In the meantime, hospitals are full while church buildings are empty, and taverns are open while churches are closed. People who have faith in God are vilified while people who have no faith in anything but themselves are glorified.

Pastor Suarez recognizes this, and has issued a clear and confident call, not just to assent or agreement, but to action. Every believer can and must respond. The hour is late, and the need is greater than ever. Multitudes are in the valley of decision, and they need guidance from another world to help them find their way out of the dilemmas they face. The answers will not come from the right or the left, from tired religious dogmas or from anything-goes nihilist tendencies. God has already provided the answer in the form of a great multitude of men and women who are not afraid and not ashamed to display their dedication to God and to their fellow man by fearless acts of courage and love.

RevivalMakers is an unmistakable call to action. Men and women of God, step forward, step up, and step out to make a difference in your world in this hour and for eternity.

CHAPTER 1

A Moment Changes Everything

Countless times in Scripture we read about a moment when the trajectory of a life is changed. A word or circumstance takes place. The rest is history.

Abram hosting God and His angels. Moses and his burning bush. Gideon, Jonah, John the Baptist's parents, Mary and Joseph—one word or event changed everything.

I've had one of those moments, and it actually didn't happen that long ago. I was speaking in early 2021 for Fresh Start Church in Phoenix, Arizona. For the sake of context, I was not familiar with this ministry prior to the invitation I received. We accepted the invite, agreed on a date, and I really didn't think about it anymore until the week before I was supposed to minister there. That week I heard God speak to my heart. It was a clear word, though I had no clue what awaited me. God told me that though He would use me to minister to His people, the invite wasn't so much for them as it was for me. He told me He was going to do something to me and show me something I've never seen before.

> When God told me He had something new, I just couldn't fathom what it would be.

Mind you, I'm a third generation Pentecostal who has a rich heritage, for which I am both thankful and proud. I was raised in weekend revivals, camp meetings, and such. Prayer meetings and "shout down" services are as normal to me as anything else in Christianity. I've been fortunate since a child to be in services where the power of God fell, countless miracles took place, and innumerable souls came into the kingdom. Therefore, when God told me He had something new, I just couldn't fathom what it would be.

It all became clear when Pastor Paul Owens introduced me and brought me to the pulpit that first night. I could hardly stand or talk. I was immediately overwhelmed by an intense touch of God, greater than I had ever felt in my life. I have been in many great moves of God, but nothing like this. It was strong, it was glorious, it was real, and it's what I've been hungering for and seeking my entire life. Then the second word of the Lord came to me: "*This is that!*" This is "that" which was spoken by the Prophet Joel. This is "that" which the church has been longing for, praying for, seeking for since the second chapter of the book of Acts. This was more than a touch; this was the manifest power of the Holy Ghost the way I always dreamed it would be when He would come in His fullness.

It took quite a while for me to regain my composure and be able to preach. They brought me a chair to sit in because I was so drunk in the Spirit I could hardly stand. I began preaching, and God interrupted my sermon with the third word that would change me. Right in the middle of my sermon, God spoke through me and said, "I don't need revival chasers, I need revival makers."

"I don't need revival chasers, I need revival makers."

And there you have it. That's the moment this book was born. That was my moment and my word, which changed everything for me. I've never been the same nor will I ever go back to what I was. I am called to be a

11

RevivalMaker, and so are you. We're not waiting for anyone else to bring a move of God to our nation, territory, or city; we're not living off of someone else's prayer life or walk with God—we embody Mark 16! Signs and wonders follow us, demons flee from us, and God has anointed us to be His hands and feet. I no longer listen to hear where revival has broken out and then chase it down to see if I can get a piece of the glory. I want to cause revival to break out wherever I am and cause others to step in. I'm fully persuaded that *greater is He that is in me.* Therefore "He through me" manifests revival wherever I go.

The church has chased revival for centuries. From Topeka to Azusa, Toronto to Brownsville, the great meetings at Rhema in Tulsa, Oklahoma to Columbus, Ohio and "Dominion" camp meetings—every time a major wave of revival has come, the multitudes have flocked to get a taste of the glory of the Lord. From Jack Coe to A.A. Allen, Oral Roberts to Benny Hinn, neither stadiums nor tents could hold the number of people who would chase and follow evangelists in pursuit of the miraculous.

This last-day revival can't simply be chased from city to city or preacher to preacher. This is something that must be manifest in every church, every city, and every believer. We need a body of RevivalMakers who live out Mark 16:17-18:

> *These miraculous signs will accompany those who believe: They will cast out demons in my name, and they will speak in new languages. They will be able to handle snakes with safety, and if they drink anything poisonous, it won't hurt them. They will be able to place their hands on the sick, and they will be healed* (NLT).

As I understand Mark 16, we don't chase down signs and wonders. Signs and wonders follow us. The early church evangelized the known world because every believer was empowered to be a RevivalMaker. The apostles were able to function in any gift of the spirit necessary in that specific moment given the need. That kind of operation of the spirit was passed down to the everyday

This last-day revival can't simply be chased from city to city or preacher to preacher.

believer so that, as Paul described, they would come in "demonstration and power." They shared Jesus from prison cells to palaces, debated the religious community, and demonstrated the power of God in their cities with the intent that they would believe.

From the down-and-out all the way to the most affluent of their society, they were the original RevivalMakers.

The state of our world requires a bold body of believers who will stand firm in the faith and become RevivalMakers by demonstrating the power of God according to the need presented. Believers with faith to pray for the sick in their offices and bind spirits oppressing their cities. Believers bold enough to stand for what is true and right when wicked rulers try to oppress our faith, yet easily approachable and welcoming enough that "whosoever will" feels welcome to join the family of God.

As I mentioned previously, I'm a third generation Pentecostal preacher. The paternal side of my family hails from the country of Colombia, which experienced a great revival directly connected to Azusa in the early 20th century. My family's conversion was supernatural. My grandfather was given a New Testament by a missionary named Joseph Knapps who was sent to Colombia by the Foursquare Church. Brother Knapps' time in Barranca Bermeja (the city our family is from) was short-lived but long enough to stir a passion in my grandfather's heart for the Word of God. He spent time reading his new Bible along with his wife and children. The Gospel as told by Mathew,

Mark, Luke, and John captivated them, but it was the book of Acts that changed everything for them. That was their moment. My grandfather read the first chapter where Jesus told His disciples to tarry in Jerusalem for the promise of the Father. The stories of the first-century church and my family have parallels—both were believing and waiting for the promise of the Father, but both had no clue what exactly the promise looked or felt like; but if God promised it, they wanted it.

My grandfather, Heli Suarez, decided that if they wanted what the first-century church had received, then they would need to do what the first-century church did. He took his family, as well as some neighbors who were equally hungry for God. They went into the countryside and camped out on a hill where they prayed and fasted for the promise of the Father. It was on that hill on the outskirts of Barranca Bermeja, Colombia, that an angel appeared to my uncle Rafael, who was eight years old at the time. The angel told my uncle where to have my grandfather go to receive further instruction. The angel told him the city (Bucaramanga), the street name and number. He said God had a servant there who would explain the rest.

> If God promised it, they wanted it.

Most of Latin America has strong roots in Catholicism, whether one is practicing or not; therefore, most have been exposed to Christ in some measure. But supernatural occurrences like seeing angels were not at all heard of. I'm sure it took a lot of faith for my grandfather to believe my uncle had seen anything and then, furthermore, follow the instructions of an eight-year-old who claimed to be having a conversation with an angel. That step of faith, that moment changed our family forever. They made the several-hours-long journey to the city of Bucaramanga and found the street name and number. Upon knocking on the door, an English missionary, who had left Great Britain to preach the message of the Holy Spirit in Colombia, answered and said, "God told me you were coming." He immediately preached the message of the Gospel as well as the message of Pentecost to my family, and upon laying hands on them, they too received the promise of the Father evidenced by speaking in other tongues. From there he journeyed back to Barranca Bermeja and preached the Gospel and the message of Pentecost to the rest of the family and community.

When I'm asked what Bible college I attended, I jokingly respond, "The dinner table." Everyone (or at least it seems that way) in our family was in the ministry. My grandmother was known for getting kicked off buses in Colombia because she'd walk up and down the aisle of the bus preaching, "Repent, you generation of vipers!" My grandfather not only received Jesus for himself and his family, he shared the message with his neighbors. The Suarezes were mockingly called "Los Aleluyas." You knew that if you got around them, you were going to hear about Jesus and the message of Pentecost.

My father went to be with the Lord seven years ago. Upon his passing, thousands of tributes were sent in from around the world. One particular letter stood out to me. It was from a man who is now a pastor of a large congregation in Colombia. In his letter he said that my father had won him to the Lord when they were both teenagers. The man said he was a wayward teen who struggled with alcohol. My father insisted in telling him about Jesus and wouldn't take "no" for an answer—so much so, that my father started visiting the bar where this young man would go to get drunk. He said my father would order Coca-Cola and became known at the bar as "Brother Coca-Cola." The man finally caved and my father convinced him to give his life to the Lord. That's my father and my heritage; there is no price too great, no measure too great. We were born to preach the Gospel.

My mother came from a devout Catholic family who genuinely revered and loved the Lord. In her teen years she was invited to a Pentecostal church where she was baptized in the Holy Spirit and introduced to Pentecost. In a moment's time her journey of life was rerouted. She worked, saved her money, and went off to a real Bible college in Minnesota—not the dinner table! She was called to ministry but was not sure in what capacity until that same missionary from Colombia who had preached Pentecost to the Suarez family was invited to be a guest lecturer at the Bible college she was attending. Her heart was touched and her moment/word from God came. She learned Spanish and set off to be a missionary's assistant in Colombia.

I could write a book simply of the miracles and stories our family has of walking with and serving Jesus, but you didn't start reading *RevivalMakers* for my biography. I say all of these things in celebration of my heritage, thankful that God placed me in this family but vulnerable enough to say I had their stories, their testimonies, and the heritage of their anointing, but I needed my own moment and word. Mind you, I think in everyone's life you will have many moments that mark you. Moses had many more encounters with God beyond the burning bush.

I try not to participate in "church bashing" simply because the critics of the church are many. I wouldn't be able to number how many messages I've heard that start with "The problem with the church...." I'm a church boy who is very aware of the flaws but still loves the church. With that said, one concern I have of the modern church is that we are content living off of the miracles of old. The residue of the moves of God of old seems to suffice. We tell the testimonies of the days of old, satisfied with what He did. My problem is every testimony, every story makes me hungry. They fill me with what I describe as a holy jealously. I don't want to simply reminisce over what God did; I want to see Him do it now. He *is* the God of yesterday, today, and forever! I'm not content simply hearing of what He did. I want to see it today! I want my grandchildren to see it tomorrow!

> This last-day revival can't simply be chased from city to city or preacher to preacher.

That special moment God gave me in Phoenix truly set me on fire to embrace what I'm to do with my life until the trumpet sounds or I see the grave. My sole purpose, be it as an evangelist or pastor, is to be a remnant of Pentecost for my generation. I'm going to be a RevivalMaker. Rather than complain about those who have walked away or tried to change the church, I'm going to be a remnant of revivals of old and demonstrate God's power to my generation.

This book is an attempt to share what I feel are necessary ingredients to be a RevivalMaker. I believe that they will work in any church, denomination, or network.

CHAPTER 2

REVIVAL TODAY

One of the most influential voices and mentors in my life is a man by the name of Morton Bustard. I first heard him speak when I was 17 years old at a church in central Illinois. It was my first time experiencing/witnessing the gifts of the Spirit in full operation. I was hooked. I wanted to know what he heard and how he heard it. Back in those days I ordered every cassette I could get my hands on of his sermons, and if he was within driving distance I was in the services. I was hungry. Within a few years he was speaking into my life and has done so ever since. There's one sermon in particular he preached in 1999 at a ministers' conference called "Earth Angels" that had an impact on me. The following is a transcription of a portion of that sermon:

> In 1885, a city was so changed after Maria Woodworth-Etter had a revival in that city, that the police had absolutely nothing to do.
>
> Amy Semple McPherson drove her "gospel car" into Indianapolis, Indiana, when there was a ban of influenza over the city. The night she drove in, it was lifted.
>
> John G. Lake—according to the government statistics between the years 1915 to 1920, Spokane, Washington, was the healthiest city in the world. The mayor of Spokane held a public commemoration to honor his efforts.
>
> Evan Roberts in September of 1904 heard an evangelist by the name of Seth Joshua plea to God "Bend us! Bend us!" This young man left and prayed the prayer, "Bend me! Bend me!" And then he began to pray for 100,000 people in Wales, and that revival was so far reaching that the miners who were robust men, but profane men, men who used to curse to the mules as they would pull the trams in

the mines. The mules were so trained to that profanity when those men went back to the meeting house and got a touch of God in their hearts, the mules had to be retrained.

Smith Wigglesworth told Lester Sumrall, "I will not get to see the greatest move of God known to mankind," but he said, "Lester, you will see it."

Lester Sumrall said, "At the turn of the century you had Topeka, Kansas, and Azusa Street, but that wasn't it." In the '50s and '60s you had the great tent crusades where ambulances were emptied out, entire hospitals were emptied out of patients, but Lester said, "That's not it!" In the 1970s you had the Charismatic Renewal. Lester Sumrall said, "That was good, but that is not it." What is happening in the world today is without a doubt the beginning of the greatest move of God known to mankind!

I agree with Smith Wigglesworth. I agree with Lester Sumrall, and my faith was ignited by Morton Bustard's message in 1999. We are living in the days that the prophet Joel spoke of.

These are the days our forefathers dreamt about and prayed for. Every sermon you ever heard where the speaker said, "One day God will do such and such," he or she was talking about *today!*

Jesus is coming back soon and His church will not be a shell of what it once was. It will have finally cracked the shell and become what He always intended for it to be—victorious, triumphant, holy, anointed, and mighty!

> These are the days our forefathers dreamt about and prayed for.

Our past serves as a foundation to build on; therefore, let me dissect some of the examples given by Morton Bustard and see how they apply to a RevivalMaker today.

> In 1885, a city was so changed after Maria Woodworth-Etter had a revival in that city, that the police had absolutely nothing to do.

Read that while reminiscing about the chants of defunding police departments, the never-ending crime wave plaguing our major cities, the addiction crisis of our time, as well as terrorism, racism, and more.

The answer to our problems is not having one more roundtable discussion. We need Holy Ghost revival! The kind of revival that brings repentance and reconciliation. Can you imagine a move of God so impacting, so far reaching that there are no illegal drug transactions; there is no racial tension; there is no breaking into homes and stealing cars? It has happened before! I've read of revivals of old that impacted communities to the degree that the entire community went dry! Bars closed up because the people only drank of the new wine!

The war on drugs has ultimately failed to the degree we now see governments legalizing the use of drugs/substances that were once deemed harmful. I have much to say of the great Aimee Semple McPherson later on, but I want to add something about her here as well. Sis Aimee was one of the very first to integrate the services she conducted, be it in a tent or church building. On one occasion, members of the notorious Ku Klux Klan were in attendance in obvious defiance to her message of integration and came with plans of retaliation, but after the service their hoods and robes were found outside on the ground. *Do it again, Lord!*

> Not every war can be won in the halls of government or on the battlefield of men— not when the war is spiritual.

Not every war can be won in the halls of government or on the battlefield of men—not when the war is spiritual. These battles must be won through intercession and revival. The solution to racism, addiction, and crime is Jesus! I'm asking God to do it again—a revival so great that the police report crime has gone down because Jesus has been lifted up. If Pastor Samuel Rodriguez was speaking on the subject, he would remind us, "Our hope is not in the elephant or the donkey, our hope is *the Lamb!*" The issues of our day do not have political solutions; if they did, we would be living a different reality right now. We must bend our knees, use the weapons of our warfare to the pull down strongholds, and look to the only One who has never lost a battle!

> Aimee Semple McPherson drove her "gospel car" into Indianapolis, Indiana, when there was a ban of influenza over the city. The night she drove in, it was lifted.

At the time of writing *RevivalMakers*, this one is of particular interest to me.

We have lived through one of the more interesting times in modern history. Bear with me, because I'm going to park here for a moment, and it may seem like this is a chapter (or book) all to itself.

History shows us that Sister Aimee's (as she was affectionately known) healing ministry was in full swing when the Spanish Flu of 1918 plagued the world. Rather than shut down the ministry, she kept on as called by the Lord. She did not stop conducting services even after she and her children were plagued with the Spanish Flu.

In her book *Aimee: The Life Story of Aimee Semple McPherson*, she even recounts preaching through sickness:

> On Saturday night, I was stricken with the ravaging disease. Somehow I got through the service. On Sunday, though I spoke at all three services, I was taken with violent chills and fever. By Monday morning I was filled with such racking pain that it was with difficulty that I sat up in bed and struggled to do up my hair for the early service. Every moment was agonizing. ...I was obliged to take a firm grip upon the pulpit in order to steady myself and keep from falling. ...Yet—I reasoned—every one of these persons present in the eager crowd was a man or a woman whose soul faced immediate eternal decisions. I must—I must—go on! I must not fail them...this was my task.[1]

It wasn't long after this that she made her famous journey from the East Coast to the West Coast in what become known as the "Gospel Car." The city of Indianapolis was still fighting the sickness. As she drove her car in, it's as if God drove the influenza out. Where is that kind of faith today?

The last few years have taken me on a journey of reconciling my faith in Christ with my admiration and association with ministers. The season has unfortunately exposed that some preached faith they did not have. Men and women I respected cowered in fear and it left me sickened, not with a virus but with sadness. Where has our faith gone? Do we not believe Jesus still heals? We need Aimee Semple McPherson-style faith and boldness now—I'd argue now more than ever!

> Some preached faith they did not have.

Another lesson Morton Bustard taught me throughout the years was to be a "pragmatic prophet." In other words, be real! One can practice caution, safety, and protect oneself from getting sick or getting others sick, but that must be balanced with the responsibility and mandate to preach and demonstrate the Gospel and power of God.

We know the church has been infected with fear these last few years. Some still are. One statement I heard time and again that bothered my spirit was, "We've never been down this road before."

In fairness, I remember thinking the same thing on March 15, 2020. But then God arrested my thought pattern and said, *"Oh really?* You who have lived through the valley of the shadow of death and uncertainty, you've never been down a similar road?" Consider the history of humanity just in the 20th century. This era is known by some as the golden era of humanity. More advances in technology, sciences, and such occurred within a generation than in any other time in human history. It was the best of times, yet it was the worst of times, as the quote goes!

The 20th century began without much of what would soon become the norm for humanity. Many ideas and concepts became reality for our lives. Automobiles had been invented in the late 1800s, but they weren't mass produced for the public until 1908. Man had always dreamt of flying but always failed until the Wright brothers' successful flight changed our lives forever. A big world became closer than ever. Submarines took us to the depths of the ocean and rockets carried humans to space.

The radio became our main staple of mass communication. Phones entered every home, and on March 11, 1945, the first computer was built. Soon the days of telegrams and the pony express would be mere memories.

Then came advances in medicine. Until Alexander Fleming discovered penicillin in 1928, almost any little bug that someone picked up was potentially fatal.

Things like television, movies, and the internet came along. The provision of pure water and effective sewage treatment, the electrification of cities and regions, and the development of modern infrastructure and roadway systems made us the world we are today. These were great days, but in the midst of the glory and greatness, sickness, war, and economic woes plagued us.

> These were great days, but in the midst of the glory and greatness, sickness, war, and economic woes plagued us.

Consider if you been born around the turn of the century. By 1906 the world had experienced the worst earthquake known to history. By 1914 to 1918 we find ourselves in World War I, which led to 20 to 40 million casualties including 116,516 Americans who died and 6 to 9 million soldiers from around the world.

By 1918 we were dealing with the Spanish Flu. It is estimated that about 500 million people, or one-third of the world's population, became infected with this virus. The number of deaths was estimated to be at least 50 million worldwide with about 675,000 occurring in the United States.

Coming out of the great pandemic we entered the Roaring '20s. Things were looking up, the economy was booming, yet America was in the middle of a violent clash between crime and police because of prohibition. Organized crime was arguably born or at the very least brought to prominence, and untold thousands were its victim during that period.

If that wasn't enough, October 24, 1929—also known as Black Thursday—followed by Black Tuesday on October 29 sent the economy into a tailspin and ten years of lack and loss known as the Great Depression. By 1932, 20 percent of the U.S. population was unemployed.

Americans persevered and things began turning around. The citizens of our country elected Franklin Roosevelt, and in his inaugural address to the United States in 1933 he encouraged the nation to come out of the Depression by saying, "The only thing we have to fear is fear itself." While the economy began turning toward brighter days, Depression-era hardships had already taken their toll on the world and led to a rise of political extremism. The most well-known was the Nazi party led by

Adolf Hitler from Germany. It was as if Americans came out of the Great Depression, took two years to breathe and relax, and then December of 1941 the attack on Pearl Harbor occurred and the U.S. was thrust into World War II. It is known as the deadliest war in *human* history. Three percent of the world's population at that time perished. We're talking about 60 to 75 million people—419,000 U.S. soldiers.

Again, go back and consider if you had been born at the turn of the century. You've already been through the worst earthquake on record, prohibition, two world wars, a pandemic, and the worst economic crisis in history—and you're just in your early 40s!

Almost immediately coming out of World War II we entered what would be known as the Cold War as the ideology of the world changed even more. An arms race began that some would argue has never completely stopped. Simultaneously, we entered into a new fight called the Korean War from 1950 to 1953. A total of 5 million perished including 36,000 to 40,000 Americans. Yet some call it the forgotten war due to the lack of attention given to it compared to the world wars of previous decades.

We came out of the war in Korea to find ourselves on the brink of nuclear war with Russia while fending off a wicked dictator in the Caribbean by the name of Fidel Castro. With the Bay of Pigs, the Cuban Missile Crisis, and the back and forth between Kennedy and Castro, nuclear war seemed imminent. The children of America practiced bomb drills, preparing for what seemed like doomsday, but thankfully it never came.

Though we didn't officially enter the Vietnam War until 1965, the truth is that in July of 1959 the first U.S. soldiers were killed in South Vietnam when guerrillas raided their living quarters near Saigon. On March 8, 1965, the first American combat troops came ashore at China Beach north of Da Nang. This war would rage into the '70s, resulting in 1.3 to 3.1 million total deaths, depending on whose reporting you follow.

I promise my history lesson is almost done and there is a point to the walk down memory lane.

At home, the sin of racism and the shame of the Jim Crow era was being confronted, leading to the Civil Rights Movement bringing about the greatest hope for equality since the end of slavery. Though too late and never enough, change and hope could be seen. The sin of hate was on full display, marked by the assassinations of John F. Kennedy, Martin Luther King, Jr., and Robert Kennedy.

By the mid-1970s, the Vietnam War had finally come to an end and the United States found itself in an energy crisis and our gravest error and sin outside of racism—the shedding of innocent blood as we somehow legalized an ungodly, inhumane practice of murder we call abortion.

In the '80s a Hollywood star turned public servant named Ronald Regan started lifting the spirits of Americans by proclaiming it was morning again.

Again, I ask you to ponder—had you been born in the early 20th century, what would your life have looked like by the '80s?

In the first two decades of this new millennium we have been marked by terrorism, war, and the advancement of ungodly agendas such as same-sex marriage.

The '80s through 1999 seem boring compared to the first 80 years, but they were filled with new challenges. AIDS, the Iran-Contra affair, the war on drugs, the beginning of the LGBT agenda, and who will ever forget the fear of Y2K or the shock of 9/11? In the first two decades of this new millennium we have been marked by terrorism, war, and the advancement of ungodly agendas such as same-sex marriage. I didn't even take time to mention other epidemics and medical scares such as polio, tuberculosis, H1N1, and others.

These last 122 years have been busy and full of chaos, fighting, hatred, and sickness! The 20th century is considered the golden era by some, yet look at what we endured! One thing seems common each time trouble comes—we look and feel unready. We have a short-term memory. We live through, get through, and then forget. When the next crisis arises we say, "We've never been here before!" That's *exactly* what people have been saying in this season, and the point of my history lesson is to say, "Oh, yes we have, and we made it!" Not only did we make it, we thrived as a people! Why would people of faith turn to despair now?

The God who did not fail us or leave us through wars, famine, depressions, sickness, and strife will not leave us now!

My book is directed to people of faith, so I must remind you that the greatest accomplishment known to mankind in the last 122 years is nothing that I have wri..tten about above. While they are great accomplishments of endurance, none compare to what really occurred—the fulfillment of the prophecy of Joel.

> *And it shall come to pass afterward, that I will pour out my spirit upon all flesh; and your sons and your daughters shall prophesy, your old men shall*

dream dreams, your young men shall see visions.

The greatest outpouring of the Holy Ghost known to mankind occurred because a small Bible school in Topeka, Kansas, earnestly prayed for the baptism of the Holy Ghost. From a young 19-year-old girl named Agnes Osman to multiplied millions of people around the world, we have witnessed what Peter preached about, Joel prophesied about, and Jesus died on the cross for!

> The greatest outpouring of the Holy Ghost known to mankind occurred because a small Bible school in Topeka, Kansas, earnestly prayed for the baptism of the Holy Ghost.

In the midst of a pandemic, the Voice of Healing movement rose up led by the ABCs of healing—A.A. Allen, William Branham, and Jack Coe—and they stopped preaching and praying for the sick. They inspired another generation of evangelists such as Oral Roberts, R.W. Shambach, and the greats still with us today.

I pray that the faith of Aimee Semple McPherson would come upon us to *drive* the Gospel into the hearts and minds of those we can reach, and by doing so *drive* the sin and hatred out once again!

Like I said, that may have felt like its own book, but I needed to get that off my chest. Now back to the assignment at hand. You may recall that I was dissecting a sermon. I'll continue on:

> John G. Lake—according to the government statistics between the years 1915 to 1920, Spokane, Washington, was the healthiest city in the world. The mayor of Spokane held a public commemoration to honor his efforts.

The relevance of our faith has been attacked on all sides by those trying to stamp it out—atheism, fake preachers, and the "woke" liberal church that has abandoned the inerrancy of the Bible and belief in the supernatural power of God. We seem to be in an endless battle with municipalities and governments, be it ungodly mandates, protests, or legislation created to trump our beliefs. We need RevivalMakers who will practice their faith with boldness. I believe that what happened to Darius, Nebuchadnezzar, and other pagan rulers of old can happen again. Though once antagonistic, they recognized the power and the authority of our God. Even if they didn't serve the God of Abraham, Isaac, and Jacob, they respected the God of Abraham, Isaac, and Jacob.

Think about it—just a hundred years ago a mayor recognized a preacher of the Gospel for his city being the healthiest there was. It can happen again! I'm praying, "God, let a revival break out where mayors, governors, and municipalities come to us and ask us to pray because they know that when we pray, our God answers."

Evan Roberts in September of 1904 heard an evangelist by the name of Seth Joshua plea to God, "Bend us! Bend us!" This young man left and prayed the prayer, "Bend me! Bend me!" And then he began to pray for 100,000 people in Wales, and that revival was so far reaching that the miners who were robust men, but profane men, men who used to curse to the mules as they would pull the trams in the mines. The mules were so trained to that profanity when those men went back to the meeting house and got a touch of God in their hearts, the mules had to be retrained.

> A revival of repentance is needed today.

A revival of repentance is needed today. We've pointed fingers far too long. We have demanded what others must do for far too long. Evan Roberts' revival prayer was simple: "Bend me."

One of the most popular songs sung by children throughout Christianity is called "He's Still Working on Me." This is one of many classic songs written by Joel Hemphill. Though I've never asked him, I don't think he intended to write it for children. When you reflect on the lyrics, I think you'll feel the same as I do. This song is for me, *right now!*

There really ought to be a sign upon my heart

Don't judge him yet, there's an unfinished part

But I'll be better just according to His plan

Fashioned by the Master's loving hands

In the mirror of His word

Reflections that I see

Makes me wonder why He never gave up on me

But He loves me as I am and helps me when I pray

Remember He's the potter, I'm the clay

He's still working on me

To make me what I need to be

It took him just a week to make the moon and stars

The sun and the earth and Jupiter and Mars

How loving and patient He must be

'Cause He's still workin' on me

Those words encapsulate the prayer of a young Evan Roberts who prayed, "Bend me!"

God must work in us first because we can do His work in the world. The answered prayer of Evan Roberts led to a sweeping revival that was a true revival of sanctification and holiness, as evidenced by the stories of the miners and mules! You could tell that they were saved!

Lester Sumrall said, "At the turn of the century you had Topeka, Kansas, and Azusa Street, but that wasn't it." In the '50s and '60s you had the great tent crusades where ambulances were emptied out, entire hospitals were emptied out of patients, but Lester said, "That's not it!" In the 1970s you had the Charismatic Renewal. Lester Sumrall said, "That was good, but that is not it." What is happening in the world today is without a doubt the beginning of the greatest move of God known to mankind!

Ladies and gentlemen, it is my opinion that the fulfillment of the prophecy of Joel was ignited by the holiness movement in the late 1800s and set in motion through that first outpouring in Topeka, Kansas. From there came Azusa, the Voice of Healing, the Charismatic Renewal, the Latter Rain, and the Jesus Movement.

Before his passing, Lester Sumrall said what is happening now is without a doubt the greatest move of God known to mankind. That was spoken during the height of the Word of Faith, Brownsville, the Baptism of Joy, and the great revival that came from World Harvest Church in Columbus, Ohio.

We are living in perpetual revival. This is no longer a trickle here and there, a move here and there—there are waves upon waves of revival and they will continue until the coming of the Lord Jesus Christ for His church! Here's what the Holy Spirit is showing me is happening in these last days.

> We are living in perpetual revival.

We've had streams of truth such as Pentecost, prosperity, faith, joy, and healing that have operated independently of each other. You belonged to one or the other. What God is doing today is a convergence of streams. The streams are becoming one river. This is a river of healing where the fullness of the blessings of God run together and anyone who jumps in receives everything the Father has promised His last-days church!

These truths, abandoned and forgotten by some, are flowing and flowing strong! The river is flowing now, and it will engulf the world with the power of God one last time before His triumphant return. The Lord spoke these words to me to release over the body of Christ:

> This is that which was spoken of by the prophet Joel when he said in the last day, saith God, I'll pour out My Spirit upon all flesh. People are hungry for that. They're seeking that. They're wondering when that will come. You tell them what I'm doing on the face of the earth right now—this is that. This is what people are praying for; this is what people prophesy about; this is the great move of God; there's not something greater coming. God says, "Don't miss My move. Don't miss what I'm doing right now because you're waiting for another wave. This is the wave that I spoke of before the great catching away of the church. This is that move."

NOTE

1. Aimee Semple McPherson, *Aimee: The Life Story of Aimee Semple McPherson* (Foursquare Publications, 1979), 145-146.

CHAPTER 3

RELIGION RESTRICTS REVIVAL

There is a unified voice in the body of Christ denouncing, rebuking, and tearing down the strongholds of religion.

When we say "religion," I suppose most immediately think we are referring to a classical liturgical style of church, but what we mean is completely the opposite. The spirit of religion has crept into the Spirit-filled church.

The descendants of "holy rollers" are too prideful for or embarrassed by uninhibited worship. A revival birthed from Quakers and shakers has now grown up and polished its image. The modern Pentecostal church has grown up and is too professional for a true move of God—the kind where we yield to Him and care more about what pleases God than what looks good on social media.

We were known for being slain in the Spirit, speaking in tongues, rolling on the floor, being caught up in the joy of the Lord evidenced by holy laughter. We danced, ran aisles, ran the back of pews, and so much more. Prayer cloths and oil vials were the standard weapons of our warfare at home. We prayed for the sick before we called the doctor, we rebuked devils and spirits, we believed in the word of faith and the power of the spoken word.

> The descendants of "holy rollers" are too prideful for or embarrassed by uninhibited worship.

"Does it really take all of that?"

I would answer and say it's an absolute *yes* for me! It takes all of that *and* whatever God wants to add to the mix! What if God has more than what you've already experienced? What if there's more than what you heard and experienced? How can any one of us say, "This is all God has" or "This is the only way God manifests His Spirit"? Such mindsets and statements challenge the sovereignty of God!

We, the modern church, would not be here today enjoying the blessing, the heritage, the real estate, and so much more that we have today had it not been for those praying saints who weren't ashamed of getting lost in the spirit and kept their spirits open to the wind of the Spirit!

We hinder revival when we forget that the things of the Spirit are only understood in faith. They are not a science. They are not understood through the wisdom and methods of man. Only by faith can the things of the Spirit be received and understood.

I spend more time debating the moves and manifestations of God with Spirit-filled believers than I do even nonbelievers. Does God really heal? Do people really get slain in the Spirit? Why are they laughing? Why are they speaking in tongues? Why are they so militant when they pray? Do you have to dance like that? Those are questions asked by the Spirit-filled, and quite frankly they leave me saddened.

My posture has always been to be open to every move of God. I don't keep God in a box of what I think He can or can't do—nor what I think He should or shouldn't do. Who are we to question the ways God manifests His power in His people?

When you think of all the years of tears, sorrow, and grief, wouldn't it makes sense that "joy unspeakable and full of glory" would come with laughter and happiness? If a small bolt of electricity could knock us off our feet, wouldn't the power of God be able to do that and more?

Do not allow the spirit of religion to turn you off to what God is doing. It may be new to you, but that isn't reason enough to not open yourself up to the moves of God. If our forefathers would have taken that posture, there would have never been a Topeka, Kansas, or Azusa Street revival.

> Do not allow the spirit of religion to turn you off to what God is doing.

A valid concern is discerning what is God and what isn't. Those filled with the Spirit will be *led* by the Spirit. The same Spirit that causes us to prophesy also gives us discernment. The Scripture admonishes us to try the spirits.

> *Beloved, believe not every spirit, but try the spirits whether they are of God: because many false prophets are gone out into the world* (1 John 4:1).

When teaching and counseling on the things of God, my position to those who come to me has always been the following: If I can give you Bible evidence for why we teach or respond in the manner we do, you must consider it. Take the Bible examples and pray to the Lord for confirmation. In that same manner, if I ever teach something or respond in a manner I can't back with the Word, *run* and never look back toward me!

There's a generation that rose up and turned their back on the Holy Spirit. They were embarrassed by manifestations of God because someone polluted the well. There was someone who dabbled in sensationalism, and rather than clean up the pollution of the well people decided to cap off the well altogether. But God has raised me up and He's raised you up in this generation to say there are wells of truth. There are wells of truth of prosperity. There are wells of truth in the Word of faith. There are wells of truth in Pentecost that cannot be capped any longer, and God has called us to re-dig those wells, open those wells so the waters of truth will flow. They'll no longer be wells but turn into streams and flow freely in the body of Christ. Our children will know the power of Pentecost, the power of the Word of faith, that generosity and prosperity and abundance is real and that if you'll yield to the Holy Ghost, God will send revival.

> If I can give you Bible evidence for why we teach or respond in the manner we do, you must consider it.

We are well aware of false prophets, abuses, and exaggerations that have taken place throughout the years. These are not new problems; they've been happening in the church since the eighth chapter of the book of Acts when Simon the sorcerer wanted to buy the ability of "giving the baptism" of the Holy Spirit by the laying on of hands. Corruption has always been around—just ask Jesus about His disciple Judas.

But it concerns me that rather than address the excess or fix bad teaching, we seem to have capped off streams of truth.

The well of prosperity was polluted by a few with their excess.

The well of Pentecost was polluted by a few with their showmanship.

The well of healing was polluted by a few snake-oil salesmen.

The well of joy was polluted by a few who were off the hinges.

The well of faith was polluted by a few who exaggerated.

Does that negate the truth of each of these wells from heaven? Absolutely not!

The response of the church should be to correct where correction is needed without abandoning the wells of revival and blessing. I still believe the people of God should prosper; how else shall the Gospel be financed? I will believe in Pentecost! I still believe in the baptism of joy! Why should Christians walk around depressed and beaten down all the time? I believe in healing! I believe in faith! We must pass down these truths to future generations and not allow religion to rob us of the fullness of God's treasure trove.

I'm tired of the holy wars. Church trouble will cause people to turn their back on revival. Religious fighting—denominations fighting against other denominations. God has no use for it. When the enemy could no longer use the vices of the world to afflict us, he fanned the flames of religion. He really doesn't care what causes us to stumble and divide as long as we don't live to our potential. Church, I don't want to be a part of it anymore. Religious politics are as wicked as national politics. We need accountability, we need structure, we need leadership, but we do not need anymore bureaucracy. The body of Christ is a monarchy with one King and of His government there shall be no end!

> The response of the church should be to correct where correction is needed without abandoning the wells of revival and blessing.

The spirit of religion will always point out the problems of the church. It will cause people to say, "No, God's not here. How can He be here when there's racial tension? How can He be here when there's political strife? How can He be here when there's infirmity?"

We push back on that spirit by speaking truth! The truth is there's nothing that the church is dealing with right now that we haven't had to deal with before. As I've written about before, the book of Acts is full of scandal, corruption, racism, lying, murder, leadership struggles, and more, but every chapter is filled with *revival!* Signs, miracles, wonders, water baptism, Holy Ghost in-fillings.

When the enemy could no longer use the vices of the world to afflict us, he fanned the flames of religion.

I come to you by the authority of the name of God. Don't let a little church trouble or a little disagreement stop you from stepping into the river of revival. Don't let some bitterness or some strife get in you and stop you from getting what God has for you. Don't allow fear to prevent you from being open to things God has for you that might be new to you! This is the day that we have been dreaming for and longing for, RevivalMakers!

CHAPTER 4

FILLED AND FULL: A RECIPE FOR REVIVAL

When I married my wife a few years ago, I foolishly asked a Southern woman if she could learn to cook a few dishes like my mother. She said, "You apparently don't know what it's like to live with a Southern woman. I'm not calling your mother." It was then that I got the revelation of Southern cooking. My God in heaven, thank You, Jesus. I never shouted over creamed corn till I met Jina. But before that revelation, I ignorantly told her, "I just need you to call my mother, because my mother uses certain ingredients that I know are good, and I looked in the cupboard and you've got some kind of pink Himalayan salt up there, and I don't do voodoo. I don't do witchcraft. I don't do pink salt; I need white salt. And don't be messing with fat and lard and butter. Don't be trying to change it and put something healthy in there. No weapon formed against me shall prosper, and that includes cholesterol and carbohydrates, in the name of Jesus."

Now, if I'm that way about my food, you better believe I'm that way about my church. I don't like it when people mess with my church. I don't like it when people take out things that are necessary and foundational for revival. God won't tolerate it! A recipe for revival was given in the book of Acts.

The church of the book of Acts was a church of prayer, consecration, and most importantly they were not merely filled with the Holy Spirit, they stayed *full* of the Holy Spirit.

> The baptism of the Holy Spirit is access to the fountain of God, to perpetual power that you can come and soak and bathe in every day.

Revival movements, revival churches, stay full of the Holy Ghost. They don't get filled one time, walk away, get their certificate, and say, "That's my Holy Ghost birthday, glory to God." They stay full, because the baptism of the Holy Ghost isn't a one-time event then you forget about it. It's access. The baptism of the Holy Spirit is access to the fountain of God, to perpetual power that you can come and soak and bathe in every day. You can come under this fountain and be renewed and be refreshed.

He is the Spirit who guides you into all truth. He's the Spirit who will give you direction. That's why I would advocate and highly suggest to you today that you don't make one decision outside of the leading of the Holy Ghost. You don't buy a car without the leading of the Holy Ghost. You don't buy a house without the Holy Ghost. My love, don't get married without talking to the Holy Ghost, because He'll lead you down paths of righteousness. He'll lead you down paths of truth, for He is the Spirit of truth.

You simply can't do life outside of the baptism of the Holy Ghost, and the church has to stay full of the Holy Ghost. I'm still a crazy preacher who thinks everyone needs the Holy Ghost. It's not Pentecostal doctrine; it's not Charismatic doctrine; it's not a doctrine of a denomination. It's Bible truth. For, He said, "I'll pour out My Spirit on all flesh." If you are flesh, you qualify for the baptism! This promise is for everyone—newcomers to Christ, adults, children, and seasoned saints alike!

This isn't optional! This isn't like a brand of toothpaste where four out of five dentists recommend it and the other one got a better contract with a different brand so he recommends that. This is unto *you* and those afar off.

I used to pray and say, "God, bring every soul to a Pentecostal church." Now, I pray, "God, send Pentecost to every church."

I don't mind what flavor of Christian you are from, nor does God, and that's whose opinion really matters. I was always a fan of Baskin Robbins and their 33 flavors. If it's ice cream, I like it, glory to God. I love God's church, every flavor of it. I'll go anywhere. I like it all. I'm a church junky; I like Pentecostal-style church and even liturgical church. I have a Baptist friend who recently reached out to me. He's open to the baptism of the Spirit, and as a result those in his circle of influence have turned their backs on him. He is stepping into something they don't really understand, but as he recounted to me, they've been praying and saying, "Come Holy Spirit, come Holy Spirit, do what You want."

> I don't mind what flavor of Christian you are from, nor does God, and that's whose opinion really matters.

Do you know what I'm praying for him and his congregation? I'm praying, "God, send a Holy Ghost baptism to that church, and God, don't do it through a Pentecostal preacher; do it through a Baptist preacher so that no one will say it was a Pentecostal preacher who influenced them."

Send the mighty baptism of power, and they too will sing the old song, *"It's real, it's real, I know it's real! This Pentecostal blessing, I know, I know it's real!"*

There are hungry souls sitting in the pews of every Christian church—from Catholics and Lutherans to Presbyterians and Methodists who are seeking after God. Some of their denomination's leaders have turned their backs on moralism, but there's a hungry generation that's crying out for God, and God will send His Holy Spirit into those movements.

> *But you will receive power when the Holy Spirit comes upon you. And you will be my witnesses, telling people about me everywhere—in Jerusalem, throughout Judea, in Samaria, and to the ends of the earth* (Acts 1:8 NLT).

I particularly like how the Amplified Bible, Classic Edition explains Acts 1:8. It says you shall become efficient, capable, and mighty after the Holy Spirit has come upon you. Spirits of insecurity and inadequacy afflict so many and hinder them from being used by the Holy Spirit. People tell me all the time, "Well, I'm just not qualified. I don't know if God can use me to revive my marriage. I don't know if God can revive my family. I don't know how God could use me." I hear what you're saying, and as a matter of fact you're right—you're not qualified. But the Holy Ghost qualified you. The Holy Ghost has made you more than a conqueror. The Holy Ghost has made you joint heirs with Christ of the promises of God the Father. It's because of the power of the Holy Ghost that you can speak and demonstrate power and victory comes. The anointing causes you to walk boldly before the throne of grace and in the presence of men.

You don't walk anywhere without the Holy Ghost. You don't go anywhere without the Holy Ghost. I submit to you that while Jesus went to the tomb alone, He didn't stay there alone. While He was lying in a tomb with soldiers all around Him, the Bible says that the Spirit of the living God raised Christ Jesus from the dead! It blew by the Roman soldiers, wiggled its way through the rocks, and the Bible says that the Spirit that raised the Son of God from the dead lives in you. Now, just think about that for a moment. If the Holy Ghost can raise Jesus from the dead, imagine what the Holy Ghost can do in you. Imagine what He's raising you up out of. Imagine what the Holy Ghost can empower you to do! RevivalMakers, stay full of the power of the Holy Ghost—stay full of consecration.

I have a friend and mother in the faith who recently turned 89 years young. Her name is Bishop Anne Gimenez. This is a powerhouse woman of God whom the Lord used to call millions to pray for the nation. A revivalist since the age of 19, you've never met anyone like her.

One day in a passing conversation she said to me, "Tony, you know that verse that says the gates of hell won't prevail against the church?"

I said, "Yes ma'am."

She said, "That was written about you."

I said, "What do you mean?"

She said, "The church is not an organization, a corporation, or a denomination. It is written, 'You are the temple of the Holy Ghost. You are the church.'"

So when Jesus said the gates of hell won't prevail against My church, He was talking about me; He was talking about you. He was talking about your family, He was talking about your children, He was talking about your marriage, He was talking about you. I declare today that the works of satan will not prevail in your life because you—His church, His ecclesia—will be great and powerful because of the Holy Ghost!

Pentecost still has a language. We still have a sound. It must be heard! The wind of the Spirit made no sound in the Upper Room; the sound came from what the mighty rushing wind touched! How will the world hear the sound if not through us? How will our children speak the language if they never hear the language?

I was raised in a bilingual home. I speak Spanish, because my father's native language was Spanish. My mother, a Chicago native, spoke English. When I spoke to my mother, I spoke English. My father spoke some broken English. When I wanted to communicate with my dad, if I really wanted to make sure I understood him and he understood me, I spoke to him in his language.

> Pentecost still has a language. We still have a sound. It must be heard!

One of the reasons I speak my heavenly language every day is because it's my heavenly Father's language! The Bible says, "When you know not what to pray for, the Holy Spirit makes intercession" (see Rom. 8:26). And when you pray in the Spirit, your Father says, "I know exactly what you're talking about. Now, here's your blessing. Here's your miracle."

Not to sound like a nerd, but speaking in tongues is similar to speaking in code, because there's one entity who doesn't understand the language, and he happens to live under your feet. You have little devils following you around with notebooks, and you're arming them with ammunition on how to attack you. You're arming the devil all week long, talking about everything you struggle with. "Oh, if he does that one more time, I'm going to divorce him. If such and such occurs, I'm done!" And those spirits hear you and subsequently attack you! Stop arming the devil with your words of doubt, anger, and strife! Speak in the language of the Spirit!

Rather than cursing your children out, start praying in the Holy Ghost over your children. What if the next time you're having a little conflict in your marriage, rather than hurling insults at each other you prayed in the Holy Ghost for each other? Your marriage might have a revival!

Language is important. The loss of language is detrimental to society. Pastor Jentezen Franklin preached a sermon years ago that impacted my life. I listen to it no less than twice a year. The sermon deals with the language of the Spirit and a warning never to lose our language. In that sermon he explained that when a people group loses their language, they cease to exist. Not their culture, not their art, not their music—it's when they lose their language that they cease to exist.

Pentecost has a language, a sound. I speak Spanish because my father spoke Spanish. I speak in tongues because when I was a kid, my mama had me wrapped in her arms at an altar praying me through to the Holy Ghost, making sure that I heard the sound of Pentecost, ensuring that I heard the sound of revival. I know things have changed since the days of old, but if we want to keep old-time power, this generation must learn the language and sound of the Spirit.

> When a people group loses their language, they cease to exist.

I don't remember every sermon I've ever heard in my life—I've heard thousands upon thousands—but I remember every altar call where God got a hold of my life. I heard the sound of travail and the language of breakthrough, and I'm making sure my kids hear that same sound and language. I make sure my kids hear me speak in tongues. I make sure my family hears me speak in tongues, not only in church but in the car and at home. I don't want tongues to be weird in my house. I want my kids to be trilingual. In my house, we speak English, we speak Spanish, and we speak Holy Ghost tongues.

RevivalMakers create an atmosphere where the Spirit can dwell everywhere they go. RevivalMakers ensure that their homes and vehicles are full of the glory of God so that when your children enter, they will have the same power and hear the same sound.

I can't control what they hear when they go to school. One particular day my six-year-old son came home from school, walking up the front yard doing some awkward and funny dance. He was singing, "Can you whip? Can you nae nae?"

> RevivalMakers create an atmosphere where the Spirit can dwell everywhere they go.

I can't control what they hear on the bus, but I make sure of what they hear in my house. I make sure of what they hear in my car. I'm making sure they hear the sounds of Pentecost, the songs of revival, the sound of the church. If music can influence them like that, I want to make sure they hear the sound of God.

CHAPTER 5

A PUSH TO PRAYER

Once after a sacrificial meal at Shiloh,
Hannah got up and went to pray.
—1 SAMUEL 1:9 NLT

RevivalMakers, there simply cannot be revival without prayer! Everything starts with prayer!

As I've told you, I'm a church kid. It felt like a church camp meeting in my house all the time. While other kids were out playing house and whatever else they played, I was in the basement of our home playing church. I'd put a suit and tie on. I'd line up my toys, and I'd preach to them and I'd pray them through. I'd line up GI Joes and I'd come and say, "Fire on your life." Benny Hinn-style, I'd knock them all out at once just with one swoop: "Fire on your life."

I water baptized Superman. He had had a bout with kryptonite, and I prayed the prayer of faith in the name of Jesus and God raised him up off of a deathbed. I'm sure you never read about that in the comic books, but I'm telling you it happened in my basement and I was there to witness it.

I would even anoint the furniture with oil. One day my mother was coming down to the basement with the laundry and she slipped on the stairs. I heard her yell, "Tony, what did you spill on the stairs?"

"Mama, you don't know who got healed right there. I prayed the prayer of faith. Mama, you don't know it but you've stepped into a miracle spot right there."

I have wonderful, vivid memories of growing up in a Christian home. Very vivid memories of what happened in our house when you got sick. We didn't call 9-1-1, we didn't get a teleconference video with the doctor. The first thing that happened in our Christian home when you got sick in the '70s, the '80s, and even into the '90s, our parents would go to the kitchen. They'd go under the kitchen sink. They had a rusty bottle of olive oil, and you were anointed with oil. They would pray the prayer of faith in Jesus' name, and the oil, the rust, and the prayer would heal you of all sicknesses. That was our first option. We would eventually go to the doctor, but that was to confirm that Jesus had already healed us.

One of my greatest memories of growing up in the house of RevivalMakers is that it was a house of prayer. We prayed about everything. Every night we would pray as a family around my parents' bed. It was similar to a liturgical style, a call and answer kind of prayer.

> We would eventually go to the doctor, but that was to confirm that Jesus had already healed us.

My parents would begin, "Lord Jesus, thank You for," and my brother and I would respond "...this day." My parents would continue, "Forgive us for," and we would respond "...our sins." They were teaching Andrew and me another language. I guess we were actually quadrilingual. We spoke English with my mother, Spanish with my father, our heavenly language (tongues), and our parents were teaching us the importance of the language that moves the heavens and earth— the language of prayer. They were teaching us how important and how vital it is to have open communication with the Father.

A particular memory that stands out to me occurred when I entered the fourth grade. I was kind of a nerd. I liked school. I was hoping to be chosen as captain of the safety patrol. The fourth grade at my elementary had two teachers. One was considered "awesome" by the other students and then there was this other teacher.

> Our parents were teaching us the importance of the language that moves the heavens and earth— the language of prayer.

Students of this era don't understand what the '80s were like. I'm telling you, teachers could be a little mean back then. Slapping desks with rulers, the occasional kicking of desks. Perhaps your memories are different, but Chicagoland was kind of rough. Well, as fate would have it, I was assigned to that teacher, the one known for kicking desks, hitting people with rulers, and getting in their face.

I went home crying about the class I was assigned to. I can still remember asking my mom if there was anything we could do about it. My mom said, "Tony, what have I taught you to do when you have a problem? We're going to pray about it."

I'm like, "All right, Mama, all right, we're going to do it." Now remember, I have a Pentecostal mama. She's an intercessor and every demon in hell is terrified of her. When she prays, things happen!

When she said we were going to pray, I thought we were going into spiritual warfare, so I began praying, "Father, in the name of Jesus, I bind this teacher with the blood of Jesus. She's under my feet right now. Satan, you are under my feet—that teacher's under my feet. I kick up the dust. She eats my dust. I go forward. No weapon formed against me shall prosper. Not that teacher, not her way."

My mom started shushing me and said, "Stop. That's not how we're going to pray."

My mother said, "Let me show you how to pray about this. Father, I thank You for Miss _____. I thank You for her life and thank You for bringing her into Tony's life. I thank You that Tony has favor with Miss _____."

I stood there with my jaw dropped in awe. I had no clue what was happening. Here I was in a crisis, needing victory over what I perceived to be an enemy, and my mom was praying the nicest prayer I'd ever heard her pray. I was like, "What in the world just happened to my mother?" She was smiling, blinking her eyes, "Lord, I just thank You. This is going to be Tony's best year in school." She might as well have recited the famous Lakewood pledge: "This is my Bible. I am what it says I am. I can do what it says that I can do. Today, I'll be taught the incorruptible, indisputable Word of God. My mind is alert; I'll never, ever be the same. Never, never, never."

I'm laughing even as I write this. I mean, it just wasn't the way we normally prayed. I couldn't figure out what was happening. I didn't need favor with the teacher, I needed victory over my foe!

She continued on: "Tony has favor with Miss _____. This is going to be the greatest year of school Tony's ever had. And she's going to be his friend. And he's blessed coming in to the fourth grade and he will be blessed going out of the fourth grade."

Then she wrote a note to give to my teacher. So I thought, *Okay. She just didn't want me to hear her tell off the teacher or rebuke her in prayer. I bet that note says, "His dad is Colombian. You better watch out. We will go all mafia on you."* And since I'm mafia, I read the note on the way to school. It was a note *inviting* the lady to come to my upcoming piano recital.

Well, wouldn't you know? That lady didn't just come to my piano recital in the fourth grade. That lady came to all of my piano recitals from the fourth grade till I graduated high school. She was at every concert. She gave me a birthday check. She gave me a birthday card. She became a friend of our family. That year literally was the greatest year of my life at that elementary school. I was elected captain of the safety patrol because of her.

Here I am, now 42 years old, still reminiscing about the fourth grade. That's a testament to the impression it left on my mind. It left a memory, a foundation in my life that when I pray, God answers prayer. When you pray, things change in your favor. My mother's prayer life really wasn't about the fourth grade alone; it was teaching me the power of prayer. That fourth grade testimony taught me that complaining does nothing to help, but prayer changes things!

> Complaining does nothing to help, but prayer changes things!

The age of social media has given us another outlet to voice our complaints and frustrations. It's become a battleground for anything and everything. I've been guilty of tweeting my frustrating and posting my complaints. In the middle of a heightened moment of frustration with things going on in our world, the gentle voice of the Holy Spirit came and reminded me, "Suarez, I can't do anything with your complaints. I can't do anything with your posts. But do you remember when you were in the fourth grade and your mother had you pray about that teacher? I turned that situation around in your favor."

It was just the gentle nudge of the Holy Spirit reminding me, and now I'm reminding you. What we need isn't more tweeting and posting. We need to pray because the effectual, fervent prayer of the righteous availeth much (see James 5:16).

I know it's cliché, but it's the truth—prayer changes things. When you pray, you have opened up direct communication with the Father in heaven, and the Bible says, "Whatsoever you ask, according to His will in His name, it shall be yours" (see John 16:23).

My kids and I enjoy a good steak, so I took them out to eat one particular evening. Everything went wrong almost immediately. We had a reservation but were seated late, the steaks came out the wrong temperature, they brought out the wrong sides—I'm telling you, everything was wrong. I may or may not have forgotten I am an ambassador of Christ filled with the Holy Ghost, and I may or may not have gotten ugly with the busboy, the waitress, and the hostess. I was getting ready to pull my phone out and leave an epistle of a bad review on the internet for this establishment. The waitress happened to walk by again, and I demanded to speak to the manager. The manager came to the table as happy and perky as can be. I dove right into my complaint and rant. I said, "You know, I've talked to the busboy, I've talked to the waitress, I've talked to the host."

I just went down the list of everybody I talked to, and he stopped me and said, "Sir, I think I know the problem."

I corrected him and said, "No, I haven't even gotten to the actual problem yet."

He interrupted me and said, "Actually, I think I do know the problem. You've been talking to all the wrong people." (I can get a sermon out of anything. I owe that man an offering—no sooner had he said it than I knew I was going to preach about this night one day.) He said, "You've been talking to the wrong people. Whatever your complaint is, you should have come to me first because they can't do what I can do. If you would've asked for me or talked to me, I'd have made sure this thing was fixed immediately."

I sat back in my chair and just started thinking, *You know, is that not the story of my life?* I'll go complain on social media, I'll complain to friends and family, and not a one of them has a solution, but the psalmist said, *"I will lift up mine eyes unto the hills, from whence cometh my help. My help cometh from the Lord"* (Ps. 121:1-2).

If you're listening, I think you will hear God say today, "I've heard your complaints. I've seen your frustration. I've read your posts. I've seen your tears. I saw all the things that you said you're going to do, but why don't you try Me? Come to Me in prayer, because when you pray in My name, I answer prayer."

> We need to be a praying church that knows how and when to call on God.

We need to get back to being not a political church or a complaining church—we need to be a praying church that knows how and when to call on God.

First Samuel 1 gives the narrative of what I'm trying to convey to you.

> There was a man named Elkanah who lived in Ramah in the region of Zuph in the hill country of Ephraim. He was the son of Jeroham, son of Elihu, son of Tohu, son of Zuph, of Ephraim. Elkanah had two wives, Hannah and Peninnah. Peninnah had children, but Hannah did not.

Each year Elkanah would travel to Shiloh to worship and sacrifice to the Lord of Heaven's Armies at the Tabernacle. The priests of the Lord at that time were the two sons of Eli—Hophni and Phinehas. On the days Elkanah presented his sacrifice, he would give portions of the meat to Peninnah and each of her children. And though he loved Hannah, he would give her only one choice portion because the Lord had given her no children. So Peninnah would taunt Hannah and make fun of her because the Lord had kept her from having children. Year after year it was the same—Peninnah would taunt Hannah as they went to the Tabernacle. Each time, Hannah would be reduced to tears and would not even eat.

"Why are you crying, Hannah?" Elkanah would ask. "Why aren't you eating? Why be downhearted just because you have no children? You have me—isn't that better than having ten sons?"

Once after a sacrificial meal at Shiloh, Hannah got up and went to pray. Eli the priest was sitting at his customary place beside the entrance of the Tabernacle.

Hannah was in deep anguish, crying bitterly as she prayed to the Lord. And she made this vow: "O Lord of Heaven's Armies, if you will look upon my sorrow and answer my prayer and give me a son, then I will give him back to you. He will be yours for his entire lifetime, and as a sign that he has been dedicated to the Lord, his hair will never be cut."

As she was praying to the Lord, Eli watched her. Seeing her lips moving but hearing no sound, he thought she had been drinking. "Must you come here drunk?" he demanded. "Throw away your wine!"

"Oh no, sir!" she replied. "I haven't been drinking wine or anything stronger. But I am very discouraged, and I was pouring out my heart to the Lord. Don't think I am a wicked woman! For I have been praying out of great anguish and sorrow."

"In that case," Eli said, "go in peace! May the God of Israel grant the request you have asked of him."

"Oh, thank you, sir!" she exclaimed. Then she went back and began to eat again, and she was no longer sad.

The entire family got up early the next morning and went to worship the Lord once more. Then they returned home to Ramah. When Elkanah slept with Hannah, the Lord remembered her plea, and in due time she gave birth to a son. She named him Samuel, for she said, "I asked the Lord for him" (1 Samuel 1:1-20 NLT).

The first chapter of Samuel's first book lays out and shows how this great prophet's life was directly connected to a prayer. His father Elkanah had a few wives, and after you read the narrative, you understand further why God only wants you to have one spouse. There's a lot of drama going on in the family with all the wives. It could've been a reality show.

His wife Peninnah was blessed with many children, which was the earmark of blessing in that time, and therefore Elkanah lavished her with gifts. Peninnah had all the name-brand bags that were out. She had the stuff you can't even buy in the store. If there had been social media in her day, she'd have been an influencer. I mean, she was the envy of everybody.

And then there was Hannah. Hannah was the one people looked at and said, "Bless her heart," not

"Blessed." One of them looked to have the perfect marriage, the perfect children, everything going right. She was the epitome of blessing. And then there was Hannah with nothing. All she desired was a child, but she didn't have what she had been hoping for.

The Bible says that they would go to Shiloh year after year to worship God. Peninnah would show up with all her blessings and children. She was like the woman who makes her mark when she walks into the church conference. She wants you to know she is there. Hannah was just happy to be there and hoped people didn't notice what she didn't have. The Bible says that year after year it was the same.

If it wasn't enough that Peninnah was blessed, she would ridicule Hannah. She'd make a mockery of her. Peninnah would bring Hannah to tears. She was sorrowful. She was even bitter because of what she didn't have.

Bible says in verse 8, Elkanah came to her one day and said, "Hannah, am I not...?" If you are married, just think about it for a minute. Her husband came to her and said, "Baby, am I not better than anything you've been believing for? Am I not better than having kids? I'm enough. Right?"

Elkanah was well meaning. Elkanah loved her, but Elkanah didn't get her. Elkanah didn't understand her faith or her pain. Everyone has an Elkanah in their life. Elkanahs are the people who try to talk you out of what you're believing God for. They quench your faith; they're cynical and just don't get it. If you're not careful, they'll talk you out of standing for God's best for your life. These are the ones who will say, "You know what? Simmer down a little bit. Why don't you just be satisfied with what you have? Why don't you just be okay where you are?"

Hannah lived between Peninnah's taunting and Elkanah's lack of faith, and if that wasn't enough, the high priest—the spirit of religion—was trying to silence her: "Lady, it doesn't take all of that."

I believe that right now in our culture, we're fighting all three spirits. We're fighting the spirit of mockery, the spirit of cynicism trying to quench our faith, and we're fighting the spirit of religion that's telling us it doesn't take all that. You don't have to pray the way your parents prayed. You don't have to fast the way they used to. You don't have to be as devoted as they were. You don't have to be as consecrated. But I tell you, the devil is a liar. One of the reasons we're in the situation

> One of the reasons we're in the situation we find ourselves in as a society is the church stopped praying.

we find ourselves in as a society is the church stopped praying.

If I may be transparent with you, I've wrestled with the Lord trying to understand what happened in this season with sickness. In my opinion, we should have had victory over the virus much earlier. We should have prayed that thing away, and it should have already gone back to the pit from whence it came. That's my opinion. I've tried to reconcile how the spiritual sons and daughters of A.A. Allen, Oral Roberts, and R.W. Schambach—raised in the voice of healing, word of faith movement, and in Pentecost—weren't able to obtain victory sooner. I felt that familiar gentle nudge of the Holy Spirit come again to me and say, "Do you remember when this happened with My disciples, and I had to take care of business, and they came back and they asked, 'Why couldn't we do it?'" And Jesus said, "This kind comes out through prayer and fasting."

We don't pray enough. The spirits of this day, they're only going to come out through prayer and fasting. We need a church that has power and authority in the Holy Ghost to say, "Get thee behind me." And when you say it, the devil doesn't laugh; he says, "Yes sir, yes ma'am," and flees.

Allow me to speak for a moment to the Hannahs reading this book. You're barren. While the Hannah of the Bible was barren of a child, your barrenness might be in ministry or business. You don't have what other people have. Your friend started a business; you wanted to start a business. His or hers is prospering; yours isn't. Your friend got married; you're still waiting, and you've watched everyone else get blessed. Everyone else has what they want. Year after year, you serve God and it's the same story. Everyone else's ministry is prospering. Everyone else's marriage is doing great. Everyone else's kids look like they just walked off the set of *Leave it to Beaver*. Everyone else is doing great, but you're stuck. Everyone else is going from glory to glory, and you're stuck.

Thank God Hannah didn't let Elkanah's criticism and Peninnah's mockery talk her out of praying and believing! I'd argue that had she given in and stopped praying, the history of Israel would look very different. Just think about it for a moment. If she gave in and said, "You know what? You're right. I don't need a child, I don't need a son. You're enough. I'm going to stop praying"—if she did that, there would

> We need a church that has power and authority in the Holy Ghost to say, "Get thee behind me." And when you say it, the devil doesn't laugh; he says, "Yes sir, yes ma'am," and flees.

be no Samuel. If there was no Samuel, there was no one to hear God's voice and interpret it to the high priest, Eli. If there was no Samuel, there was no one to lift up their voice as a prophet to help Israel recover the Ark of the Covenant. If there was no Samuel, there was no one to anoint King David. Do you get the picture? A woman's insistent prayer life changed the history of Israel. Hannah made a decision to not just keep crying about her situation or complaining about her situation—she *prayed* about her situation.

First Samuel 1:9 arguably changes Israel's history. It says, *"One time..."* (GNT). She cried many times. She got bitter many times. She was hurt many times, but *one time* she got up and prayed. She said, "Oh God, answer my prayer. Give me a son."

> A woman's insistent prayer life changed the history of Israel.

Here's a difference between Hannah and a lot of us. Hannah was anguished, Hannah cried, Hannah was bitter, but she prayed. Life will hurt. Oh yes. Life hurts at times. Everyone has situations and issues and reasons to be bitter and be full of hurt and anguish and pain. But it's what you do with those feelings that makes the difference. What I've learned about God is that He sees our hurt. He sees our anguish. He sees what's going on, but the Bible teaches us that the only thing that God answers is our prayer. He doesn't answer our tears. He doesn't answer our pain. He doesn't answer our anguish. We have to turn those things into prayer and then the effectual, fervent prayer of the righteous availeth much (see James 5:16). Hannah took these hurts of life. She took the ridicule. She took Elkanah's criticism and Eli's mockery, and she turned it into a prayer life.

There is a RevivalMaking proverbial Hannah reading this book who needs to know how close you are to breakthrough. Don't stop praying, don't allow anyone or anything to quench your faith!

> *Don't worry about anything; instead, pray about everything* (Philippians 4:6 NLT).

And First Samuel 1:19 says, "The Lord remembered her plea" (NLT). Not her tears, not her pain, not her sorrow—the Lord remembered her prayer.

So to those Hannahs reading, here's the word of the Lord for you. You've watched everyone else get blessed, you've watched everyone else prosper, you see everyone else doing great. You've waited, you've watched, you've cried, you've hoped, you've anguished, you've been confused and perplexed, and at times you've said, "What shall I do?"

Pray. Pray without ceasing. Pray until the bitterness goes away. Pray until you can no longer speak in your native tongue and you start praying in the Spirit. Pray, pray, pray until God answers your prayer. And I promise you that when God hears your prayer, He'll honor it, He'll remember it, and He will answer your prayer.

> What if you're one prayer away from the miracle?

What if you're one prayer away from the miracle?

RevivalMakers, let us return to a lifestyle of prayer that shakes the earth and brings heaven to where we are.

CHAPTER 6

HOLINESS PROTECTS REVIVAL

Sadly, there is no way to discuss the subject of holiness without it becoming controversial. There are two sides to every coin, as they say, and I want to attempt to speak to both sides here. An "anything goes" spirit has afflicted the modern church. Perhaps it's just the pendulum swinging from extreme legalism in the past to extreme liberalism today, but we must come back to a place of true biblical holiness that is pleasing and acceptable to the Lord.

In raising us up as RevivalMakers, God has chosen us to be the visible image of our invisible God to the world. When your neighbors see you, they see Jesus—or at least that's our hope. There is a responsibility over the life of every RevivalMaker to not live simply for yourself. Your life is a living sacrifice that testifies of the glory of our God to those around you. However, the way you live your life will speak to those around you of the effectiveness of the Gospel. Beyond that is our chief responsibility to our Lord and Savior. We cannot disrespect the sacrifice of Calvary and dishonor the blood of the Lamb by living lawless lives. There is a standard of righteousness the Lord expects us to hold up and live by.

> Your life is a living sacrifice that testifies of the glory of our God to those around you.

While I don't think it would be pragmatic of me to go issue by issue, I do want to speak to a few that are heavy on my heart before I go on. The acceptance of alcohol in the Spirit-filled church is now widespread, and I believe it has opened doors we never intended to open. I can tell you stories of preachers not being allowed to get on their next flight due to intoxication. I know of ministers gathering for drinks after a "successful service" and even dabbling with other vices, excusing it in the name of relieving stress. I do not believe God is pleased and, more so, I believe He's brought judgment upon us.

Please hear me—I'm not writing this from a posture of perfection, but rather in pursuit of pleasing my God. While we agree that there is no official biblical prohibition on strong drink, there certainly is regarding drunkenness. The line is blurred and argumentative when it comes to the question, "What is drunkenness? Is being tipsy the same?" I personally find that the best practice is simply to abstain from it all.

I felt the Lord speak to me recently regarding drinking. It impacted me enough that I felt I needed to take time in this chapter to specifically speak to the subject. This is what He said to me: "Tony, I've given My children new wine, yet they seem to desire their wine more than Mine. It hurts My heart to see them prefer their drink over Mine. When they drink of the new wine, there is joy unspeakable and full of glory, there is healing, and there is life. But their drink leads to death."

Again, this is my conviction, and perhaps you feel differently on the subject. Therefore, you must follow Christ as He leads you. But we must be honest with ourselves that what was once deemed a behavior or a lifestyle becoming of the ministry really does not exist anymore. It doesn't line up with the admonitions of God in the Old Testament to his priests and in the New Testament to the fivefold ministry.

Friends and acquaintances are walking away from ministries, their families, and their marriages because of sin. They never intended for it to get to this point, but there was a portal, a gateway that was opened. I believe one of those doorways that we should consider completely closing again is that of drinking. Before you accuse me of judgmentalism, consider why I'm so passionate. I was on a long-haul flight to the other side of the world several years ago. The flight attendants were handing out champagne and mimosas to everyone in our cabin. When offered a glass, I obliged and was ready to partake when God spoke to me. I heard Him ask me, "Is there nothing you have to give up for Me anymore? Can you simply do whatever you want to do and live however you want to live? Is there nothing sacred to you anymore?"

I quickly took my hand off of the glass and left it on the tray. I carry a strong conviction to this day, a conviction not birthed out of a rule book or because of a family tradition, but because God placed it on me. Ladies and gentlemen, God is still speaking! Are you listening to what He wants you to do or not do? I pray that we can hear God's voice, not through

> Friends and acquaintances are walking away from ministries, their families, and their marriages because of sin.

the mouthpiece of a denomination or the sound of approval or disproval of family, but the real voice of God that speaks to individuals.

I want my life to please God. There are boundaries of protection that every believer should have in their life. That doesn't mean every issue is salvific, but it does mean I'm trying to honor the Lord in every area of my life—not to avoid hell, but simply to please Him.

In the next chapter you'll read about the necessity of *living ready*, so I don't want to be redundant, but for the sake of this discussion on holiness, God has shown His bride infinite mercy and grace. He's given us room to clean up our lives and get things right, and I'm sure He will continue to do so. But it's time, church—it's time to get right.

> God doesn't demand much from us, but He does demand that we pursue a holy life.

We know too much, we've heard and read too much to be playing with our salvation. God doesn't demand much from us, but He does demand that we pursue a holy life.

We need to be born again. The entire third chapter of the book of John is a sermon all in itself. It's very commonly taught and preached from within Spirit-filled churches and really is the narrative of a conversation with a certain religious leader named Nicodemus who came to Jesus one night. He was in awe of the miracles and the wonders that were done at the hands of Jesus. He realized that there was something special about Jesus—He must be more than just a simple man, and yet it went against what Nicodemus had been taught.

Here again, we see the conflict that the spirit of religion causes for those who are following after God. Nicodemus could sense that there was more than what he'd been taught, but to find more he needed to abandon certain areas of his religion. This might have cost him family and friends. It was so serious that he didn't meet with Jesus by day but rather under the cover of night. Nicodemus was in pursuit of God, so much so that he was even willing to go against the religious norms of his family and community. In this secret meeting, Jesus brought up the necessity of being born again.

The story gets interesting because Jesus' statement left Nicodemus dumbfounded. The phrase *born again* is common to us *now,* but at the time Jesus said that to Nicodemus, it was the first time in Scripture that phrase was ever used. So it was a shock to Nicodemus when Jesus said, "You must be born again." It didn't even make sense. He couldn't compute or comprehend what was being said.

At times I wish we could hear live recordings of these Bible stories because I'd love to hear the emotion and reaction in Nicodemus' voice to what must have sounded like a preposterous proposition from Jesus—to be "born again." Nicodemus asked, maybe sarcastically, "What do You mean I have to be born again? I'm an old man. How do I enter back into my mother's womb and be born again?"

Jesus explained, "Unless the man be born of the water and of the Spirit, he shall not enter into the kingdom of God" (see John 3:5). We understand what that means. If you're reading and have already been born again, please allow the evangelist in me to take a moment and give someone else an opportunity to enter the kingdom!

If by chance you are a Nicodemus who has picked up this book and you haven't been born again, please let me tell you how easy it is. Humbly I tell you the same thing Jesus spoke to Nicodemus, "You must be born again."

> I'd love to hear the emotion and reaction in Nicodemus' voice to what must have sounded like a preposterous proposition from Jesus—to be "born again."

It is not enough to just say, "I like Jesus and agree with His teachings." There is a response needed from us. Jesus encouraged us in John 3:5 to be born of water and spirit—human birth and spiritual birth. Our spiritual rebirthing is in response to the finished work of Calvary. When the question was asked in Acts 2, "What shall we do?" in response to Peter's sermon, Peter answered and said, "Repent and be baptized, every one of you, in the name of the Lord Jesus Christ. And you shall receive the gift of the Holy Ghost."

We understand that the work of salvation begins at faith in Christ but doesn't end there. It continues through repentance and turning away from a sinful lifestyle. And because of our repentance and our faith in Christ, we're then compelled to be identified with Christ in water baptism. And because we are baptized into the body of Christ, we have the promise of the Father, which is the Holy Spirit.

> The work of salvation begins at faith in Christ but doesn't end there.

I had a man ask me how many steps I thought it took for an individual to be saved. Of course, the question was posed by a religious man trying to trap me in a response that he could later use against me. I responded, "Well, that depends how long you're going to live!" Jesus didn't call you to take a step; He called you to walk with Him. It starts at faith and progresses through repentance, water baptism, and God baptizing you in His Spirit, but it doesn't stop there either! It continues through steps of victory, prosperity, holiness, and one day a trumpet is going to sound and we'll stop walking as we fly away to meet Him in the air!

So as great of a promise as the new birth is, we need to realize that the new birth isn't the end—now it's time to live *for* and *in* Christ! Could you imagine babies being birthed and left in the maternity ward? The baby isn't born simply to be born; it is born to live life to its fullest. It's the same in the kingdom. A soul is more than simply a number we use to celebrate our successes in reaching the world. A soul deserves discipleship and the opportunity to have the fellowship with Christ that Adam and Eve abandoned in the Garden of Eden.

There's more. The Bible calls us to live as a living sacrifice, *holy* unto the Lord, pleasing, and acceptable. The Scripture goes on to say in the book of Hebrews that we're to, *"Follow peace with all men, and holiness, without which no man shall see the Lord"* (Heb. 12:14). The Old Testament proclaims, "Be ye holy for I am holy, sayeth the Lord" (see Lev. 11:44-45; 19:2; 20:7,26).

I've heard sermons, teachings, and concepts about holiness since as far back as my mind can remember. Depending how long you've been a Christian, I suspect you've heard about holiness as well. Many times, holiness comes across as something negative and religious. Holiness is thought to be as nothing more than a religious rule book or legalism; it's a religious scorecard for others to judge whether you're really good or not good enough in the kingdom of heaven.

If we're being honest, the scorecard we keep isn't normally about us but about others. We judge others' salvation simply by the clothes they wear or the style they keep. The reality is that what religion has boiled holiness down to is not the holiness the Scriptures speak of. The Bible describes holiness as beautiful. Any depiction of holiness that includes judgment and condemnation is not the true picture of holiness. Holiness is the nature of Christ. It's not a mere list of rules. I would argue that true holiness is the polar opposite to religion's manmade rule book.

> Many times, holiness comes across as something negative and religious; it's a religious scorecard for others to judge whether you're really good or not good enough in the kingdom of heaven.

Holiness does not equal perfection. As you study the Scriptures and you look through your Bible, you'll find men and women of God who were considered holy by God, and they had messes in their lives. They had situations in their lives. They made mistakes in their lives, but they loved God enough to acknowledge their sin, repent, turn away, and most importantly seek refuge in the holiness of God. In other words, they recognized their shortcomings and the mistakes they made. They confessed their faults and were conscious that there were many reasons God should be disappointed in them or walk away from them. Yet the cry of their hearts was to fix, correct, and make right the things that were displeasing so they could draw closer to God.

The journey on the highway of holiness is not so much to focus on *what* you're walking away from but *who* you are drawing closer to. I'm walking in holiness to draw closer to Jesus, and the closer I get to Him, the more I'm made in His image. The more I'm perfected by the Spirit, the more I am like Christ. And one day—and it won't happen here on earth—but one day in my pursuit of Christ, the trumpet is going to sound, the eastern sky is going to part, the dead are going to be raised, and we're going to go to meet Him in the air. And when we reach that blessed place, we will be holy, just like Him, because we pursued Him. And because we pursued Him, we pursued His character. He called us out of the world. He called us into His marvelous light so that we could present our life as a pleasing sacrifice. It's a life that is trying to simply please the Lord. That's what holiness is.

One knows a marriage is in trouble when the focus is on the obvious boundaries that should be in place in marriage. Can you imagine being married and day in and day out discussing the importance of not cheating on your spouse? I'd say that your marriage is in crisis if that were the case. There are obvious guardrails to marriage, but the focus should be on growing closer in relationship with one another. When coming together, the focus isn't on the rules but the relationship.

> The journey on the highway of holiness is not so much to focus on what you're walking away from but who you are drawing closer to.

Shouldn't that be true about our relationship with the Lord? Religion is infatuated with rules and legislation. God gave Moses Ten Commandments, but by the time Moses got done preaching to Israel, there were another 600-plus rules in the rulebook. Our incessant focus on legislated religion shows that we do not trust the Holy Spirit, for if we truly believed in the power of God's Spirit, we would trust Him to lead people into "all truth" as the Scripture proclaims.

"Tony, we need people to live right!" I hear you, but there's something greater than religious legislation—it's the conviction that comes from someone who's so in love with Jesus they're consumed in relationship with Him to the degree that they are living to please Him. Religion and legalism teach us to walk on eggshells to not anger the Lord, lest He punish us. That is a pathetic way to live our lives. I'm not living in fear of His anger; I'm living in the fullness of His joy and love. Someone reading may say this contradicts my earlier admonition regarding drinking. I would counter and say, consider the spirit in which it was written. I wrote the warning not to condemn you to a sinner's hell but from a place of personal conviction and humility, desiring that we do our best to show Jesus to the world and protect our lives and homes from the toils of the enemy.

> When coming together, the focus isn't on the rules but the relationship.

We've raised generations of unrighteous theologians who can quote Scripture and have knowledge of God, but the truth is they do not know God. They know about Him, but they don't know Him. They know all the dos and the don'ts of their religious persuasion and do not know the very character of God. They know their persuasion, but they don't know the person. Holiness is not so much about what you're taking off or what you're going to stop doing, but it's about putting on Christ. It is about what you get to do. I get to serve the Lord. I get to live in the kingdom of heaven. I get to be a part of the body of Christ. I get to be redeemed. I get to be restored. I get the favor of God. I get the blessing of heaven. That's what holiness is to me. Holiness causes the favor of God to come over me and flood me with blessings everywhere I go.

A pastor friend of mine from Los Angeles named David Zuniga said it this way, "When the enemy can no longer use the things of the world to bind you, he'll start using religion. He'll start using things of the church, and he doesn't care what binds you— as long as he has you bound, as long as you're ineffective, as long as you're in defeat, as long as you're walking with your head hanging low. He doesn't care what it takes as long as he has you bound." The enemy has used the subject of holiness to bind people. I know that doesn't seem possible and you might read that statement and think, "Tony must've missed that line in proofreading. It doesn't sound right," but he certainly has. The enemy has manipulated and redefined a blessed message into a way to keep people bound from serving the Lord. He's tried to make it something negative that would cause us to run from the house of God and run from pursuing a relationship with God. He makes it seem as if it's this unbearable yoke that comes on us and, "I'll never be good enough and I'll never qualify and I can never do it."

That is completely opposite to the message of the cross—the message of the Gospel of Jesus Christ. If you think you can do it, then you're already delusional. You can't do it. There's nothing you can ever do, there's nothing you can ever give, there's nothing you can sacrifice that will ever bring you salvation or bring you holiness. But the good news is you don't have to do it. He already paid the price. He did it so that you could walk in His holiness.

> Holiness is not a yoke to bear; it's not depressing— it's a blessing.

Holiness is not a yoke to bear; it's not depressing. If you are practicing something in your life that you call holiness and it feels like a yoke and burden, I humbly submit it's simply that—a man-made weight. Holiness isn't a yoke, it's a blessing. It's freedom, not confinement.

Several years ago I felt the Lord had spoken to me and said, "Remind My people how they're positioned." He said, "Remind them that I go before them." And it is written, "If the Lord be for you, who can be against you?" (see Rom. 8:31). He said, "Remind them that goodness and mercy follow them and that the angels are around them."

I said, "What's goodness and mercy doing back there?"

He said, "Goodness and mercy are picking up everything that My kids lost along the way."

Every RevivalMaking parent reading can understand what goodness and mercy do. I like watching parents who have younger kids. I get nostalgic for when my kids were young and also thankful I'm not there anymore!

I was at one of my kid's ball games watching the parents of toddlers running all over the place. Their kids were dropping toys, cups, food, and even dropped blankets, and the parents were just walking behind them, and they'd pick this up and they'd pick that up and they'd pick this up. The kids were oblivious to what they were losing along the way, and had it not been for Mom and Dad picking it up along the way, those items would've been lost forever!

The child has no concept of how much that blanket cost or the cost of the toys they easily lose. The child didn't have to pay the price, so they don't always feel the same responsibility to the item. But to the parents who are still paying off their credit card bills filled with kid items they say, "I know that that costs $12.99 and that costs $2.99 and that costs

$24.99. So though you drop it, I'm going to pick it up because I paid for it and I know you're going to want it later."

Goodness and mercy are walking behind you because that anointing, that ministry, that calling, those blessings that you have, you didn't pay the price for them, but God so loved you that He gave His best. He gave His only begotten Son. And because He paid the price, He said, "Not only am I not going to let you lose it, I'm not going to let the enemy take from My kids what belongs to them." So goodness and mercy are walking behind you. If you walk in holiness, pleasing the Lord, you have the Father in front of you, goodness and mercy behind you, and you have the angels of the Lord all around about you. Now I understand why the Bible says that, *"No weapon that is formed against thee shall prosper"* (Isa. 54:17).

> Goodness and mercy are walking behind you because that anointing, that ministry, that calling, those blessings that you have, you didn't pay the price for them, but God so loved you that He gave His best.

Man-made holiness teachings encourage and promote a false performance-based gospel that is not of God. I recall a baseball tournament my son Kohl played in not too long after we lost his mother to cancer. It was a Mother's Day baseball tournament, and I knew it would draw high emotion. I wasn't sure if we should even play, but he was insistent that he was going to play in memory of his mom and make her proud in heaven. I was nervous for him just watching the pressure he was placing on himself to play as if she were in the stands. As you can imagine, the pressure got to him. He dropped a ball here and there and struck out twice, but do you think that's what I posted on social media? Do you think that's my lasting memory of that tournament? Absolutely not. I posted all four runs batted in, the two doubles, the triple, and a few singles he hit. I have videos of both stolen bases, including when he shocked the opposing team by stealing home to win the game for our team. I have memories of the highlights!

Remember, I can get a sermon out of almost anything, including a baseball tournament!

I was watching him play and I said to myself, *You know what? That's what it's like living for the Lord under the pressure of man-made religion"* We place an unhealthy and unnecessary pressure on ourselves to live up to a certain standard that can't be obtained. The pressure causes us to drop the ball and not live up to expectations. I don't believe anyone purposefully wants to dishonor God; we want to please Him. But just like a kid in a ball game, sometimes we mess up. Many times this pressure is there because of God's representatives that preached or taught performance-based religion. We say, "I don't want to let God down," but in reality we don't want to let that representative down. That can be family, friends, ministry—anyone who has led us to think this way of God.

Do you, for one minute, think when the game was going on or ended that I was focused on the things that went wrong? No! In fact, when he did drop a ball here and there I noticed that immediately he'd look my way. What was he looking for? Approval and acceptance. Every time, he found the rowdiest and loudest fan in the bleachers saying, "That's okay, Kohl! You got this! Keep it up buddy! Shake it off! Forget it and move on!"

> We say, "I don't want to let God down," but in reality we don't want to let that representative down.

I pray that you're released from the pressure of competitive, unbiblical, performance-based religion. Your heavenly Father *loves* you and is proud of you! He's not focused on the dropped balls as much as you are. (Mind you, nothing I'm writing is to condone sin, but rather to remind you not to stay there.)

Your Father in heaven celebrates you for standing for Him and for righteousness in the midst of an unrighteous culture. He celebrates the goodness that you're living in. I know you messed up along the way. I know you've tripped along the way. I know there are times when you've sinned along the way, but I want you to know in heaven's highlight reel, it doesn't have all your blunders and your mistakes. The Bible says that He takes those and He throws them into the sea of forgetfulness. And when the enemy comes to accuse you, He says, "I don't know what you're talking about." He brags on you the way you brag on your own children, and in the same manner you pull out your phone to show videos and photos, I believe Jesus pulls out His heavenly memory reel and says, "You must be talking about someone else. Look at My boy. He's praying. He's living for God. He's reading his Bible. He's doing his best. This is My son in whom I am well pleased."

> Your Father in heaven celebrates you for standing for Him and for righteousness in the midst of an unrighteous culture.

I think the true pursuit of holiness is not for the adulation of men and religious systems but rather to hear that same voice that spoke over Jesus and said, "This is My Son in whom I am well pleased." I believe that if you and I pursue God, we will find holiness that pleases Him. I want God to be pleased with my life. I want God to be pleased with the way I walk and the way I talk and the places I go and the decisions I make and the actions that I engage in. I want God to be pleased. And I recognize that, at times, I'm going to make a mistake and I'm going to make a bad decision. But if I want to please God, I'll pursue Him and His holiness. And this is not the primary reason, but if I pursue His holiness, favor follows me. I'll be flooded in the favor of the Lord.

There are different Bible characters who'll stand out to me at different times and I'll just really dive into their lives. One of those in recent years has been Daniel. I can't really identify with the Melchizedeks and Enochs of the Bible. Anyone who is so perfect and hasn't had to live through anything and they go automatically to heaven—I don't get them. But you give me a David, a Rahab, a Samson—I get them. I understand.

Studying Daniel's life, I have understood a lot more about myself and how I should try to walk with the Lord. This man was taken out of what should have been a blessed land and into captivity. He was taken into Babylon and forced to engage in a culture that was completely opposite to what his faith taught him, and attacks came against him.

You know this story well, but what stands out to me is Daniel 6:4; it's what his enemies and his critics had to say about him. Daniel's enemies, when they spoke about him, said, "He's faithful, he's responsible, and he's trustworthy. The only thing we can attack is his faith." Daniel lived a life of holiness, integrity, and honesty to such a level that when the enemy wanted to attack him, there wasn't a skeleton in the closet for them to pull out.

Now, I'm not implying I've reached "Daniel status," not by a long shot, but since this came to me my daily prayer is, "Oh God, touch my mind, touch my heart, touch my vocabulary, touch my actions. God, touch everything about me so that I can please You to the extent that, and I know it sounds wild, but I want hell to say of Tony Suarez, 'He's faithful, he's responsible, and he's trustworthy.' When the enemy does decide to attack me, the enemy will have to say like Daniel's enemies, 'The only thing we can attack is his faith.' But it is written, when the enemy comes in like a flood, the Lord will raise up a standard against it" (see Isa. 59:19).

> As you live a life trying to please God, not leaving any area for the enemy to use against you, the only thing he can use against you is your faith.

As you live a life trying to please God, not leaving any area for the enemy to use against you, the only thing he can use against you is your faith. And if the only thing he can attack is your faith, you're in a good place today because it is already written, it is already declared, it has already been established from the foundations of the earth that you are more than a conqueror through Christ Jesus and *"greater is he that is in you, than he that is in the world"* (1 John 4:4). You are a victor today.

I want to know God. I want to know the sound of heaven. I want to know the language of my God. I want to see what He sees. I want to know Him, walk with Him, talk with Him, listen to Him, and I'm willing to do whatever it takes for God to be pleased with my life.

There is an old song written by the incomparable Lanny Wolfe that embodies the cry of my heart as I pursue God:

> There's a voice calling me from an old rugged tree
>
> And it whispers, "Draw closer to Me
>
> Leave your world far behind
>
> There are new heights to climb
>
> And a new life in Me you will find"
>
> For whatever it takes to draw closer to You, Lord
>
> That's what I'll be willing to do

And whatever it takes to be more like You

That's what I'll be willing to do

Take the dearest things to me

If that's how it must be to draw me closer
to You

Let my disappointments come

Lonely days without the sun

If in sorrow more like You I'll become

I'll trade sunshine for rain, comfort
for pain

That's what I'll be willing to do

Oh, for whatever it takes for my will
to break

That's what I'll be willing to do my Lord

That's what I'll be willing to do

For whatever it takes to draw closer to
You, Lord

That's what I'll be willing to do

And whatever it takes to be more like You

That's what I'll be willing to do

That's my heart's cry. Whatever it takes, that's
what I'm willing to do.

As I've mentioned, I'm a church kid who loves church, namely the Pentecostal church. I openly don't follow every custom of previous generations, but in fairness neither did they follow every custom of the generation that preceded them.

Every generation is guilty of passing judgment on the upcoming generation for not doing everything like them, forgetting that there was grace to change and grow for them. If we really adhered to everything taught to us, I wouldn't be sipping coffee while typing right now. You wouldn't have a radio or television by which to hear gospel singing and preaching, and we wouldn't take medicine for a headache. But we submitted to Hebrews 6:1-3 and went on toward perfection growing in Christ.

All that said, I honor our founders and our heritage. We need to be careful to not be found disrespectful of what old-timers used to preach, just because we might not preach it the same way today. Those men and women of holiness did what they did for the most part because they wanted to please God. Sometimes maybe they pushed it too far, maybe some of it seems unnecessary, but discern their heart—it was out of this burning desire, "I want to please God. I'll give up whatever I have to give up. I'll stop going wherever I have to stop going. I'll stop talking to whomever. I just want to please God."

God gave you the baptism of the Holy Spirit to help guide your walk. Here's the good news about living in holiness—the Spirit of the Lord will illuminate your path, so you know where to walk and where not to walk. It'll give you the mind of Christ, so you know what to do and what not to do. You're not alone in this. It takes the Holy Spirit reigning in your life. Hebrews 10:16 says, *"This is the covenant that I will make with them after those days, saith the Lord, I will put my laws into their hearts, and in their minds will I write them."* Every Spirit-filled believer who allows themselves to be led of the Spirit will have the laws of God written upon their hearts. It'll be in their mind. The Holy Ghost will teach you the difference between right and wrong. The Holy Ghost will quicken us and warn us when we fall into error.

> The Spirit of the Lord will illuminate your path, so you know where to walk and where not to walk.

I have been blessed with a godly mother. She was a missionary to Colombia, and she is an apostolic mother to many. She helped build an orphanage in Ethiopia, and she served faithfully by my father's side for close to 40 years, pastoring in Chicago while building many, many churches. She still travels the world preaching the Gospel, and she is gifted at reaching young people and being a mother to them. I used to tell my youth group friends, "If my mom and dad are tough on you and don't let anything slide, it's because they genuinely love you. They treat you like they treat Andrew and me because they love you like a mom and dad."

I remember my mom's passion was that the children of the church would know the Word of God. She taught us to memorize Scripture. You needed to know the Word of God. You needed to know the character of God. You needed to know God. And like we all have probably done, sometimes we would walk away; we would backslide. That's what we used to call it in the church. We'd walk away from the things of God.

I remember two specific testimonies of young people who walked away from the Lord for a season. When they came back and got right with God, they testified the same account with tears streaming down their cheeks. They said, "When we were out there in the world and we were doing things that we knew we shouldn't do, the Word of God would echo in our minds through the voice of Sister Anne. Sister Anne's teachings would echo in our hearts and in our minds, and we would be trying to do something we shouldn't and it was as if we could hear Sister Anne preaching, 'Be holy. You don't belong to the world. You belong to God. You've been bought with a price.'"

That was the natural voice echoing what the Spirit voice says. It was the blood calling them back home. The blood of Jesus cries out on our behalf today that that sacrifice not be in vain. That the death on the cross not be in vain. That the whipping post not be in vain. That the blessing of the Holy Spirit not be lost on you from you. This is your salvation. This is your blessed life, simply by pursuing Him.

REVIVALMAKER'S PRAYER

Oh God, Your body stands today at attention and cries out to You. Make us holy. Purify us, sanctify us. Make us the body that You desire and call for us to be. God, as Your church, which You have ordained as a house of prayer, we pray a corporate prayer of repentance. We repent, God, for engaging in things we shouldn't be in and for allowing the enemy at times to distract us from where we should be focused. We cry out to You today and say, "Make us holy." We're passionately in pursuit of You. We want to please You. We want that same voice that was

> The blood of Jesus cries out on our behalf today that the death on the cross not be in vain.

spoken over Jesus to be spoken over us, "This is My son. This is My daughter in whom I am well pleased."

Now by the authority of the Holy Spirit of God and by the power of the name of Jesus, I rebuke the spirit of condemnation that has laid its claws in the minds of certain believers, telling them that they can never live in holiness, they can never please the Lord, that their life can never be right. I take authority over that spirit and I cast it out in the name of Jesus of Nazareth. Spirits of insecurity, of unrest, not being able to forgive yourself, I take authority over them right now in Jesus' name. And I speak by the authority of heaven and declare that we are more than conquerors through Christ Jesus. Hallelujah.

> Your Father is waiting for you in heaven, not to judge you but to welcome you!

Hebrews likens our walk with God to a race, and I would remind you today that this race is not about who starts. It's not given to the swift. It's all about who finishes. Your Father is waiting for you in heaven, not to judge you but to welcome you! The first words you're going to hear Him say are *well done! You made it!* All that matters at the end of the day is that we make it to heaven and that we hear the Father say, "Well done, My faithful servant."

CHAPTER 7

RAPTURE GENERATION: OUR BLESSED HOPE

I've recounted many stories of my childhood in this book—stories engrained in my mind that shaped me to be who I am today. My brother and I were not allowed to leave the house in the morning without first praying for my mom. The thing that usually varied between us was our time of repentance. He had a much shorter list than I did!

We did not miss prayer time even if it meant missing a bus. Prayer time was important, and we were taught to make time for it every morning. You could try to make excuses, such as, "Mom, listen,

I'm going to miss my class or game. I got to go get the bus."

She'd quickly respond, "Well, you're going to miss heaven if you don't pray." That sounds extreme to some, but it was the *normal* discipline of every Christian family to value prayer and Bible reading.

My mother cared more about our salvation than anything else! Every morning Andrew and I would recite the following Bible verses before we left for school.

> *Blessed is the man that endureth temptation: for when he is tried, he shall receive the crown of life, which the Lord hath promised to them that love him. Let no man say when he is tempted, I am tempted of God: for God cannot be tempted with evil, neither tempteth he any man: but every man is tempted, when he is drawn away of his own lust, and enticed. Then when lust hath conceived, it bringeth forth sin: and sin, when it is finished, bringeth forth death. Do not err, my beloved brethren* (James 1:12-16).

When I wasn't doing my best, mom would really focus on verses 15 and 16 with me. There were times

I went trembling to school! I didn't want to miss the rapture! I didn't want to go to hell!

When I was growing up, every song and most sermons talked about the coming of the Lord. Movies were made about the coming of the Lord. There was a healthy fear, a needed respect for the coming of the Lord. We were trying to live ready. We knew He could come back at any moment. We lived as if the trumpet could sound at any minute. So if you sinned, cussed, or anything else, you were quick to repent in case the coming of the Lord was that same day!

> We were trying to live ready. We knew He could come back at any moment.

Even as children we were taught to consider our steps and actions. I think everyone who has ever done something wrong knows the feeling of, "What if my dad finds out? What if my mom finds out?" But there was a generation that reminded themselves, "Oh my God, Jesus is watching. He knows what I think, what I say, and where I go."

I can remember my parents dropping me off at school events and admonishing me, "We might not be there tonight, but Jesus is there. The Holy Ghost is there. Jesus is watching you." It developed the fear of the Lord, respect for our God. This wasn't to intimidate us to walk in perfection—that's impossible. It was simply a reminder to live ready!

Ladies and gentlemen, Jesus is still coming. We don't hear about it as much anymore, but RevivalMakers live ready and prepare for the coming of the Lord!

For many it is as if we have decided that He must not be coming. Therefore, some will live any way they want to live. We want to do whatever we want to do, but I am here to admonish you. Be alert and be careful, because if you could see what's transpiring in heaven I think you would see Gabriel polishing the trumpet.

> Be alert and be careful, because if you could see what's transpiring in heaven I think you would see Gabriel polishing the trumpet.

I'm of the opinion that Gabriel has already warmed up and is ready to sound the alarm. He's put the mouthpiece to his lips and is ready, but the merciful hand of the Lamb of God has cupped the bell of the rapture trumpet and said, "Not yet. Not yet. Not until My children are saved. Not until their spouses are saved. Not until I get one more out of the clutches of sin." Jesus reminds Gabriel, "I did not come to condemn the world. I did not come to put them in hell. I went to earth to bring them to heaven. Don't sound the alarm yet.

There are still more souls to be saved. I want to make heaven crowded. So hold back on the trumpet, because there's still more to be saved."

I write to you out of a holy conviction that the time is short. Heaven is getting crowded, and more and more nations are receiving the Gospel, fulfilling Mathew 24:15.

As the people of God we need to live ready, from the youngest convert to the oldest saint. This is not time to play around. It's not time to waver into other philosophies or turn our backs on what we know to be true. It's time to plant our feet and preach this Gospel and stand in this truth and be ready. The winds are blowing, but they are not going to knock us over. Change has come, but we are already established and we are waiting for the coming of the Lord.

> It's time to plant our feet and preach this Gospel and stand in this truth and be ready.

I'm an evangelist of the Lord Jesus Christ and I'm compelled to preach, write, remind, and warn you—ladies and gentlemen, Jesus is coming again, and in my opinion it's not hundreds of years down the road. It's not thousands of years down the road. Very soon the trumpet is going to sound and we better be ready. We won't have an excuse to say, "Well, no one told me and no one preached to me and no one prepared me." The warning and alarm is right here on the pages of this book to you. RevivalMaker, you must get ready and, if necessary, get right because Jesus is coming again soon! This is the urgency that compels RevivalMakers to preach fervently, give generously, and live like there's no tomorrow! We're too close to the coming of the Lord to play around now!

I fancy myself a student of human behavior. I like to see how people react. You can tell a lot about a person by their reactions. We recently commemorated the 20th anniversary of 9/11, and I reminisced and remembered how we reacted to that moment in history. Most of us who were alive for that time remember where we were. We remember what we were doing when the Twin Towers were attacked and subsequently fell. I remember my mom calling me. I had just woken up to go to work. I worked at a little suit store and I needed to make my way there. She said, "Before you go, you better see what's happening on television."

I never did get to the suit shop that day. In fact, I didn't go back for about four days because everything shut down, everything closed. The malls were empty and the ball fields were empty, but there was one place that was full. It was the house of God. It didn't matter what denomination. It didn't matter what flavor of Christianity—from Catholic to Protestant, every synagogue, every house of faith was full, even those of other faiths. We called for a special prayer service that Tuesday night and I can still remember my father's reaction as he walked out into the sanctuary. I remember my dad walking out, walking with his head down, and when he looked up he was startled. It was because our church was completely full on a Tuesday night. There were even folding chairs. I mean, there were people everywhere. I still can hear my father. He grabbed the mic and his first words were, "Well, I thought you all worked on Tuesdays."

We had never had a crowd like that for a midweek service. It was packed out. And that's the way it was day after day after day. People ran to the house of God. We turned to prayer and we were seeking God. During this time, our President addressed the nation and told us that in order to show victory to the terrorists who attacked us, we needed to return back to normal. We needed to go back to what we always did, the way we always did things. That way we would show the enemy they didn't win. We couldn't show them that our lives had been affected by their actions.

We understand what his heart was for the nation at the time, but I wish things had not gotten back to normal. Within a week's time, the church had emptied again and the sports stadium filled up. The malls were filled and we forgot about the house of God once again. We forgot about prayer. We forgot about the necessity of turning to God in our moment of need. Just like that, we went right back to normal.

Here we stand, twenty-some years later, having come through—or going through, depending on how you see it—an interesting season. Life has been altered, and I wonder what will happen this time? Will we simply revert back to normal or will we never forget the lessons we've learned?

> Will we simply revert back to normal or will we never forget the lessons we've learned?

I've often wondered why we weren't ready for 9/11, because the reality is we simply weren't ready for a terrorist attack the morning of September 11, 2001. That was the last thing on our minds even though there had been signs of an impending attack. Just like with 9/11, when this season that we've been living in came, we weren't ready. Now, we've had a pandemic of sorts every 100 years, give or take. So in my frustration, I have often wondered to myself, *Why didn't anybody write a book after the last one? Why didn't someone leave a blueprint* Well, it turns out they did. There are even articles and historical records warning us about how to take care of one another in case of a pandemic. Each historical account tells us the same thing—it does not matter how much you prepare. It does not matter how much you warn. Humanity is never ready.

In the spiritual sense there is no better example than that of the 100 years leading up to the great flood. Noah was preaching and he was warning the world to prepare. He was building and he was preparing, but no one listened. They would ridicule him. He sounded like a crazy prophet. He sounded like he was off his hinges. He was a wild man, but he kept building and he kept preparing and he kept prophesying and he kept preaching. The Bible says in Matthew 24:37, *"But as the days of Noah were, so shall also the coming of the Son of man be."*

> It does not matter how much you prepare. It does not matter how much you warn. Humanity is never ready.

RevivalMakers, we sound crazy to the world. We look foolish to some, but don't stop building the ark! Don't stop building up God's church. We are preparing a generation for his coming. Our message is like that of Noah, and it is time to get right. Love and learn the Word of God. Sadly, history repeats itself, and just like it happened in the days of Noah, there are going to be people knocking at the doors of the church one day soon saying, "Let me in, let me in, let me into church!" They will be flocking to the house of the Lord, but it will be too late.

> *Now learn a lesson from the fig tree. When its branches bud and its leaves begin to sprout, you know that summer is near. In the same way, when you see all these things, you can know his return is very near, right at the door. I tell you the truth, this generation will not pass from the scene until all these things take place. Heaven and earth will disappear, but my words will never disappear* (Matthew 24:32-35 NLT).

We make sure our house is secure. The last thing we do before we go to bed is we go check every door. We check every window. We make sure that we have our car keys. We make sure that our house is completely secure. When I'm traveling, I can look on an app and I can see if the alarm is on or off. The Scripture admonishes us to protect our spiritual house in the same manner! There is a thief seeking to steal, kill, and destroy your salvation! He has made it his life's evil mission to destroy you. He's looking to steal your salvation. He's looking to kill your faith. He's looking to quench the fire of the

Holy Ghost, and he comes at you from the left and from the right.

The Lord is saying that in that same way that you protect your house because you do not want anyone to take your jewelry, money, and valuable possessions—protect your soul even more! Say to yourself, *I'm going to make sure that my salvation is secure. I'm not going to let rebellion get into my heart. I'm not going to let bitterness get into my heart. I'm not going to let depression or sin or the things of this world get into my heart. Instead, I am going to make sure that I stand firm in the faith because we're too close to the hour when the trumpet is going to sound!*

> There is a thief seeking to steal, kill, and destroy your salvation! He has made it his life's evil mission to destroy you.

You need to understand that this is what it says in the Scriptures:

> *So you, too, must keep watch! For you don't know what day your Lord is coming. Understand this: If a homeowner knew exactly when a burglar was coming, he would keep watch and not permit his house to be broken into. You also must be ready all the time, for the Son of Man*

will come when least expected (Matthew 24:42-44 NLT).

Let me be clear. We don't live in fear of the coming of the Lord—it's our blessed hope! I just want to be ready and prepared. I have some family members up there whom I'd like to see again. There are some people I'd like to talk to up there. I'd like to see David worship God in person, live and in color. I have a hunch my Father will challenge David to a dance-off, and knowing my Father, David has his work cut out for him. I'd like to meet Peter and talk to him about the upper room. I'd like to sit down with Elijah and talk about miracles. I'd like to meet the one known as the weeping prophet, Jeremiah, who no longer weeps but has a smile on his face because God has rescued the exiles of Israel. I'd like to see Daniel and ask him to tell me what it was really like when the lions were coming around him and he stood firm in his faith. And more importantly than all of those Bible heroes, I want to see the face of Him—the Holy One. The One who loves us so much that He gave His only begotten Son and said we are worthy of the blood of the Lamb of God. That's what this is all about. I

> We don't live in fear of the coming of the Lord—it's our blessed hope! I just want to be ready and prepared.

don't want to miss my opportunity to see my Lord and Savior.

I fly somewhere between 275,000 to 300,000 miles a year on an airplane. The TSA agents and the gate agents all know me at the airport. Do you think that just because they know me and I know them, it gives me the right to show up whenever I want to show up? If that plane is taking off at 9:12 a.m., I can't show up at 9:17 a.m. and say, "Why didn't you let me on the airplane? You know my status, you know me, you know I was supposed to be on the plane!"

If I ever did that I'm sure they would respond and say, "All of that's great, but you knew the plane was taking off and you should have been here. You of all people should know better! You should know to be here on time!" Ladies and gentlemen of the faith in Christ, please hear my heart's cry. When that trumpet sounds, be ready, and tell others to be ready as well.

Now that I'm in my forties, I've turned into somewhat of an emotional guy. As I travel with Jina around the nation, I'm approached by young adults, who have families of their own now, who were called to the ministry, were water baptized, or were filled with the Holy Spirit in youth camps I preached at 20-plus years ago. It means everything to see that 20-plus years of ministry were not in vain. There is fruit from the sacrifice. Souls weren't just touched for a moment. They're still living for God, and now they're preparing others to be ready for the coming of the Lord!

The Bible likens the coming of the Lord to a wedding—the marriage supper of the Lamb. We, the bride of Christ, are going to meet our kinsman Redeemer. The One who loved us enough that He came for us. You didn't have to seek Him. He sought you out. It's common in classical Christianity to say, "I choose Jesus" or "I said yes to Jesus. I have accepted Him." While we obviously do not have a problem with any of that, we must be aware that we never chose Him. He chose us. He chose you and me while we were yet sinners in rebellion. Knowing the end from the beginning and the beginning from the end, the God of eternity saw us and loved us enough to save us. He chose you. And so we're getting ready for the marriage supper of the Lamb.

> We're getting ready for the marriage supper of the Lamb.

Do you remember the old wedding adage, "Something old, something new, something borrowed, something blue"? It's applicable to the soon coming meeting with our Lord and Savior.

SOMETHING OLD

Remember and hold on to what got you here! The Bible says to not remove the ancient landmarks.

Remember where you came from! I love the church. I'm thankful to be Spirit filled. We can't ever stop preaching the power of the Holy Ghost. We can't ever stop praying for the sick in Jesus' name. We can't ever stop preaching what got us to where we are. The foundation remains the same.

SOMETHING NEW

While I need to hold on to some things of old, I must also have something new.

> *So let us stop going over the basic teachings about Christ again and again. Let us go on instead and become mature in our understanding. Surely we don't need to start again with the fundamental importance of repenting from evil deeds and placing our faith in God. You don't need further instruction about baptisms, the laying on of hands, the resurrection of the dead, and eternal judgment. And so, God willing, we will move forward to further understanding* (Hebrews 6:1-3 NLT).

RevivalMakers cannot be stagnant people, stuck in what God did in the past, and miss what He's doing today. The great revival is double rain! The former and the latter rain together! The harmony of old and new coming together. A marriage will not be successful if one or both individuals reject the notion of two becoming one in hopes of preserving an identity that really is no longer there. Change has occurred; therefore, embrace and live in the new!

SOMETHING BORROWED

If you've been walking with the Lord long enough, you know that every good and perfect gift cometh from the Father above (see James 1:17). I don't own anything, but He has given me access to everything. He's a good Father. He's not stingy. He's not tight with what belongs to Him. And if we go and ask Him for any good thing according to His will and in His name, He said it shall be ours. We must embrace and remember that truth. We're really not owners of anything; we're stewards of everything. Treat everyone and everything like they are the Lord's possession because they really are. One day the Owner of everything is going to come and ask, "What did you do with that life? What did you do with that ministry? What did you do with that talent I gave you?" because it's time to be tried with fire.

> He's a good Father. He's not stingy. He's not tight with what belongs to Him.

It convicts me so much. I remember being in a camp meeting that T.F.

Tenney was preaching. He said, "Your work is going to be tried by fire." And he said how sad would it be to spend your whole life doing something, and when it goes through the fire it turns into stubble because it was never the work of God. You didn't accomplish what you could have with the resources God made available to you.

Friends, when my works are tried through the fire, I want them to come out like gold. Maybe there could be some imperfections. It could have some dents. It could have some scratches, but I want to know that what I did had eternal value.

SOMETHING BLUE

Blue is the color of love. The body of Christ needs a revival of love from one to another. We don't just gather a bunch of strangers to worship together every week. You are my brother. You are my sister, and I'm not going to fight with you because I have a Father in heaven. If He's anything like my earthly daddy was, He gets real ticked off when His kids start fighting with one another. We need a revival of love. I can't make it without love for God, for the body of Christ, for

> I can't make it without love for God, for the body of Christ, for humans at large, love for the kingdom and love for myself. We need love.

humans at large, love for the kingdom and love for myself. We need love.

You say, "Love for yourself? That's kind of weird." No, I have to love myself enough to not be lost. I have to love myself enough to get in the Bible and get in prayer and be ready.

CHAPTER 8

EXPECTATION

God takes pleasure in expectant faith. He likes hungry children who come back for more and more. Earlier this year, I'd come home from traveling and had been gone longer than usual. Whether right or wrong, you get used to eating in restaurants every day. I was really craving some home cooking, and I happen to be married to one of the best cooks who's ever stepped in a kitchen. Jina is the kitchen RevivalMaker! Obviously she is much more than that, but let me tell you, she owns that kitchen!

I'd been gone several days in a row, and on the flight home I was bored. You can only watch so many YouTube videos or work on so many things before you run out of things to do on an airplane. On the flight home I just began to ponder. I pondered on one of my favorite subjects—food. I wanted some home cooking.

When I got home, Jina asked if I wanted to take everyone out to eat. I told her honestly that I would rather just eat something at home. I began to relay my airplane think tank session to Jina. I told her that I'd been thinking about what my favorite food was, and I had made an official decision. My favorite food is Jina's potato soup. No sooner did I say it than she burst into laughter, thinking I was lying. I told her I was as serious as can be! She knows I'm a carnivore, so she naturally assumed my favorite food would be steak.

I said to her, "Think of all the steakhouses we've gone to. Have you ever heard me ask for another steak?"

She said, "No."

I said, "But every time you make that blessed potato soup, I eat like eight bowls of that soup. I gain seven pounds in one day, eating that soup. I don't do that with any other food at any other place!"

Jina started to believe me and said, "You really like it that much?" Well, guess what was on the stove *the next day?* Not one pot but *two* pots of potato soup! Later that night, as I was diving into my eighth bowl of soup, she said to me, "It dawned on me that you might be telling the truth. When I remembered how you act when I make the soup, something in me said, 'If he likes it that much, I'm making sure he has soup.'" She took pleasure in that.

Again, I can turn anything into a sermon, including a story about my gluttonous infatuation with Jina's potato soup. Yes, there are spiritual applications here as well! Think how your heavenly Father feels when He knows you delight in His blessings and in His ways. He takes pleasure in pleasing His children. When he sees that pleasure exemplified in your praise and your worship, when He sees that you're satisfied in Him, that you're happy, that you're full of joy, that you're thankful, it causes God to give more and to pour out *more* of His goodness upon you. Gratitude provokes blessings.

> He takes pleasure in pleasing His children.

I crave the things of God as well as the blessings of God. That hunger for Him causes God to show His power and goodness to me.

I began this book by discussing a moment I had with God in early 2021 at Fresh Start Church in Phoenix, Arizona. I had another one of those moments in Chicago in 1999. I was a younger preacher and I was hungry for the miraculous. I had grown up seeing God do miracles in our church. I had seen people baptized and filled with the Holy Spirit. But just like I talked about in the potato soup story, there was this hunger for more. Every time God moved in our service, I was never satisfied—I wanted more. I said, "What else, what else can You do?"

We would have these great moves of God where we were literally drunk in the Holy Ghost. Young people would carry us onto the bus after youth camp because we were just flat, sloppy drunk in the Holy Ghost. And I remember sitting on the bus thinking, *What else can You do?*

I was not satisfied that He had just moved in a service; I was expecting and hoping that He would move on the bus home from youth camp. Sunday morning service, I'd come in with this wild expectation: "God's going to do something." There was just this hunger for more of the Lord. And back when I was a kid, most Pentecostals didn't have televisions. And if you did have one, you didn't tell anybody that you had one because it was the one-eyed devil and you weren't supposed to have one.

> I was captivated by and hungry for the miraculous. I needed to know if it was real or fake.

Thankfully, we had a "monitor" (a TV without cable) that I could rig with paperclips to pick up channels.

I used to watch Christian television for hours on end. I'd watch those services with a holy frustration stirring up on the inside of me. I'd watch those healing crusades where 20 and 30 wheelchairs were brought to the front emptied. In a moment, people were healed here and there, and scores of people lined up, ready to testify of how God had healed them, God had delivered them, and God had done miracles. I was captivated by and hungry for the miraculous. I needed to know if it was real or fake.

When I got to the stadium in Chicago that day I saw a lady in a wheelchair with an oxygen tank. I saw her husband help her out of the car and wheel her into the stadium. God allowed me to see that because He was going to show me something later in the service to prove to me this was really Him.

The Holy Spirit filled the stadium as the people began to praise and worship God. During that time of worship, I heard a lady shriek. I turned around to look and it was that lady from the parking lot. She was disconnecting the tubes that were in her nose. She was disconnecting everything from the oxygen tank. I watched her pull herself up and stand up out of the wheelchair, her husband crying. And I saw her begin to lift her legs and walk, completely healed. Nobody laid a hand on her. Nobody spoke the word of faith to her. She was just healed in the presence of God. And I watched as she and her husband just started celebrating.

I heard a shout come from the other side of the stadium. I don't know exactly what healing they received, but it was obvious something miraculous was happening. Pastor Benny said, "Yes, Lord, do it again." Miracles started happening like popcorn all around the stadium. No one had to pray. No one had to ask it, because in the presence of God anything and everything is possible.

> Nobody spoke the word of faith to her. She was just healed in the presence of God.

God took me to that service to encourage my faith and change how I approach God with my needs. That service confirmed what my father had always taught me about praise and worship—when we praise God up, blessings come down! God inhabits the praises of His people. When He comes, every blessing and benefit comes with Him! It's only a praise away! At a miracle crusade, I saw it. It was like the praise went up like a magnet and literally pulled heaven down to the earth. The atmosphere of the miraculous was created through praise and worship, and all of these miracles started popping up and taking place all over.

Overwhelmed by everything God was doing, I stepped into the lobby of the arena. There was a lady beating on the door demanding she be let into the service. Apparently the arena had reached maximum capacity and they weren't letting anyone else in, but this lady was persistent. She yelled, "Let me in! Let me in! Don't you understand? If I get in there, I'm going to get a miracle!" That moment marked me. This lady was not coming with her fingers crossed hoping that God would move on her behalf. She was convinced—if I can just get in the room, *I know I will be healed!*

> She didn't have hope. She had expectation. They showed up confident— if I can just get in that room, I will be healed.

She didn't have hope. She had expectation. So did multiplied thousands who attended and received miracles that day. They showed up confident—if I can just get in that room, I will be healed.

That service changed my life because that day God revealed to me the highest level of faith that exists—expectation. They expected to get a miracle. They expected to get healed.

It changed my perception of how I approach the Father. For years I've been coming bashful, timid—"If You would, would You please heal me? Would You please bless me? Would You please make a way?" But the Bible says to come boldly before the throne of grace. He is your Father and we are His children. RevivalMakers expect God to answer. RevivalMakers expect to see miracles. RevivalMakers expect revival. We're not hoping, we're not praying that it might happen—we're looking in expectation! That's how you should approach every service—expecting there will be a moving of the Spirit, expecting revival will break out.

I'm fully aware of the times we're living in, the trouble that has surrounded us, the opinion of our naysayers in the world regarding Christianity. But here's where I stand today—like the woman trying to enter the crusade in Chicago, I'm knocking, I'm pressing, I'm pushing to get into the presence of God. I just know that in His presence anything is possible!

I expect miracles. I expect healing. I expect revival.

There's an old song that not everyone remembers, but it's the song of my heart for this season:

I hear the sound of abundance of rain!

God's going to pour out His Spirit on all man!

Like the days of old

Revival's coming again

I hear the sound of abundance of rain!

CHAPTER 9

AMBASSADORS IN CHAINS

There are two specific verses where the apostle Paul refers to himself as an ambassador, each written in different contexts. In Second Corinthians 5:20 we read the words of an often-frustrated apostle—frustrated with the religious establishment already taking form in the early church, but a free man nonetheless. This is the commonly used reference to being an ambassador for Christ, but I want to focus on another instance found in Ephesians 6:19-20:

> *And pray for me, that words may be given to me when I open my mouth, to proclaim boldly the mystery of the good news [of salvation], for which I am an*

ambassador in chains. And pray that in proclaiming it I may speak boldly and courageously, as I should (AMP).

As you are probably aware, the majority of the New Testament was written from behind prison walls, but have you ever considered the word picture given here by the apostle? "Chained ambassadors"? Doesn't it seem to be an oxymoron to be a *chained* (confined, bound, imprisoned) *ambassador* (sent, go, envoy, representative, surrogate)? The older I get, the more the world changes, the more I believe we can relate to being "chained ambassadors" for Christ as Paul was.

Our Gospel message, while still the Good News (glad tidings) for all people, is certainly not the most popular message. It bucks against the desires of the flesh; it challenges the corruption of the systems of the world; it shines light in the darkness, and in doing so foils the plans of the enemy. It's for those reasons that the enemy of our soul stops at nothing to stop the spreading of the Gospel message as well as creating roadblocks to prevent believers using their God-given authority to influence this present world. Thus the attacks we see from classrooms, courthouses, places of business, and all the way through government.

Our Gospel message, while still the Good News for all people, is certainly not the most popular message. It bucks against the desires of the flesh; it challenges the corruption of the systems of the world; it shines light in the darkness, and in doing so foils the plans of the enemy.

Being a Bible-believing Christian who believes Jesus is the only way to the Father and the infallibility of the Bible, places you in the class of extremism these days. You are almost guaranteed to be censored, ridiculed, and delegitimized. Taking a Judeo-Christian stand will most likely get you kicked off committees, barred from boardrooms, and subject you to ridicule rather than reverence.

But when has it been any different? All you have to do is go back to the Garden of Eden and see how the enemy was present to keep Adam and Eve from walking in communion with God. This story is played out time and again. From Pharaoh to Jezebel, the rulers of the philistines to Herod, the plan of God is always faced with resistance.

My father hailed from Colombia and lived most of his life under the oppression of socialist rebel armies fighting a never-ending civil war with the government. Later came the danger of the infamous drug wars that besieged the country from the '70s forward. He warned me a day was coming when "they" would come for our Bibles and attempt to prevent us from gathering to worship. He talked about bonfires where communist soldiers would gather and burn all the Bibles in villages, and drug lords would threaten pastors to hide drugs in their buildings. If the pastor did not take the bribe, they were told to leave immediately or face the risk of death.

Preaching the Gospel of Jesus Christ caused my father to be physically attacked. One time he was stoned until he was unconscious and essentially left for dead. His crime was preaching and singing the good news of Jesus Christ. I heard stories of smoke bombs being thrown into the windows of little churches to stop the saints from singing. They kept preaching, they kept singing, they kept making disciples. Through persecution and even full-on attack, they advanced the kingdom of God.

They were ambassadors in chains.

My father warned us that as time went on, these would not simply be the stories of Colombia but could be or would be the story of every believer. Hearing his passionate pleas to respect and honor the Word of God did not always compute to a child and teenager of the '80s and '90s who didn't live through any real persecution. Now, I consider my father a prophet. He knew these days were coming. He foresaw a day was coming when the government would go as far as to arrest pastors in the United States for conducting Christian services. He foresaw a day when the Bible would be bullied, burned, and buried as fables rather than revered and respected as the Word of God.

Thus we too are now ambassadors in chains.

We have been called to be light in the darkness, and now the reality of what it will take to eradicate the darkness of hell is settling upon us. The call of the Gospel is not to practice our faith in private, sing alone, and hide who we belong to. We are called to show forth His marvelous works, testify of Him, and announce He is coming back!

> We are called to show forth His marvelous works, testify of Him, and announce He is coming back!

Easier said than done, at times. In the turbulent world of local to national government, it would seem to the natural eye that any hope for morality and integrity is lost, but RevivalMakers see things differently. The decadent state of our culture causes a holy anger to rise up from believers because we know things didn't have to be this bad, we didn't have to get to this place of immorality, but here we are. But aren't we tired of simply being angry Christians? This is when RevivalMakers show up.

Back about a decade or so ago I was invited to attend a political gathering in Washington, DC. The cause was something dear to my heart. I was frustrated about where our nation was headed, but I didn't know what to do with my anger other than simply complain. A clergy friend invited me to go with him to Washington, DC, and at first I turned him down and said, "Things never change, why bother?" He kept after me to attend and asked me if I had ever heard of Sam Rodriguez or heard him speak. I had not. He shared a video or two that was available on the internet. I had never heard a Pentecostal leader of Hispanic descent speak with such authority and clarity to the issues of our day. I don't like to make comparisons and I especially avoid it these days, but I will tell you that 11 years ago when I heard Pastor Sam (as I refer to him) speak, I said, "He's the Latino MLK."

"You are what you tolerate."

"Silence is not an option."

"Today's complacency is tomorrow's captivity."

"We will never sacrifice truth on the altar of political expediency."

Those are just a few Pastor Sam quotes that resonated with me and that I've never forgotten. Fast-forward to the event I referenced in Washington,

DC. There was more than a quarter of a million people gathered. Mind you, it was a political event, so every faith was represented. Pastor Sam was one of several faith leaders who was asked to pray. Usually at events like this, at least when it comes to faith representation, everyone has a "Kumbaya" kind of an attitude—including the faiths that don't know that particular hymn. One is asked to speak/pray in generalities and never make a comment/prayer that would seem divisive or cause a believer of another faith to feel ostracized.

While the concept may be noble, Christians are to be peacemakers but never sell out the truth of the Gospel—as in Pastor's Sam quote about *never* sacrificing truth on the altar of political expediency. Several faith leaders came to the podium and prayed nice, polished, generalized prayers to "higher powers," and one even prayed to nature. Pastor Samuel stepped into the mantle of the prophet Samuel when he took the podium. When he prayed, he prayed in the name above every name, the name of Him who was, is, and is to come, "My Lord and Savior *Jesus Christ.*" He was a living example of the apostle Paul's call for us to be ambassadors for Christ. He was not ashamed of his Savior and fulfilled Colossians 3:17, which says everything you do in word or deed, let all be done in the name of Jesus Christ.

Heaven touched the earth that day in Washington, DC. I felt it. It wasn't too long after that when Bishop Anne Gimenez connected me to Pastor Sam and I ended up working for and with him. One of the greatest honors of my life has been walking with Pastor Sam from the church house to the White House. From the baristas at Starbucks to the Oval Office, he showed me what it meant to be an ambassador for Christ through his consistent walk with God and willingness to pray with anyone. I sat in more than one meeting in which politicians literally pleaded with us to let down our conviction regarding the sanctity of life in lieu of other political agendas/legislation. Every time, every single time, their call to compromise met a brick wall called integrity. We walked away from many a meeting frustrated with the humans we had met with but satisfied that we pleased God rather than man.

> Christians are to be peacemakers but never sell out the truth of the Gospel.

It has been Pastor Sam's influence on my life that convinced me that one could be an influential Spirit-filled leader in today's society. When I first started working with Pastor Sam, the DC scene was mainly filled with non-Spirit-filled Christian leaders. In private we were encouraged to tone down the Pentecostal/charismatic rhetoric. It was implied that for one to have influences, one needed to be somewhat bland in their statements, prayers, and op-eds when it came to controversial issues. Mind you, this was 10 to 15 years after leaders such as Pastor Rod Parsley had written *Silent No More* and lit a fire of passion for Spirit-filled believers to get involved. Pastor Parsley raised his voice and in turn raised a generation of bold leaders to take a stand on issues such as life, marriage (as defined in Scripture) and preaching liberty to the captives (be it from slavery in Sudan or the clutches of sin). Rod Parsley demonstrated that true revival starts in the church house but must reach every house, including the house of government.

Not to be redundant, but the assumption was that the only way to stay "in the fold" in DC is to compromise. Pastor Sam has done something I have not seen done since Billy Graham. He has never compromised his convictions and yet has not lost the opportunity to speak to whoever occupies an office. It's actually quite biblical and prophetic. When we walk into the room as ambassadors of the Lion, the Lamb, and the Dove, the elephants, the donkeys, and the serpent come under subjection to the authority given to us. I've seen the most controversial figures in American politics struggle to find words while meeting with us and end meetings asking Pastor Sam to pray or for counsel for their personal lives.

On the one hand we fulfill the role of ambassador while the media, including religious journalists, seem to do their best to keep us chained. The serpent is shrewd and intentional in his attempt to silence the true church. He also apparently doesn't have a good memory. Paul did more as an ambassador in chains than he did without them.

In one of the darker times of humanity, God has raised you and me up to be ambassadors—sometimes in chains, other times without, but always ambassadors of truth and righteousness. In the age of cancel culture and censorship, the ability to spread the true Gospel might be more difficult, but our calling compels us to go forward preaching and teaching the Gospel. I know many are tiring from the constant fight, even amongst some who claim to be followers of Christ yet are deceived by a false social gospel of allegory and fables rather than truth and righteousness. We are tired of being buffeted from every side, ridiculed, and questioned, but ambassadors keep on—even when in chains. The mission is too critical and the King we represent has saved us from too much to let a few devils scare us off.

RevivalMaking ambassadors speak truth to empower not just civic leaders but religious leaders as well. The shame of the age for me is to see people raised in the things of God who have abandoned truth for a lie. They have been given over to demonic teachings such as universalism, the gospel of inclusion, the LGBTQ agenda, and the disregard for the sanctity of marriage. Anything goes. This, in my opinion, might be the church's greatest fight because these voices already had a foot in the door. It's a spirit, not a person we fight, but that spirit has gotten hold of some popular singers, musicians, athletes, and preachers. They're not silent about their issues! They're not bashful to bash the truth! Therefore, we can't afford to be silent either. Words have power, so we must arrest each of their lies with truth. We must embrace the role of ambassador, not just to society and our community of faith but also to our families. How will our children know what we stand for and why, if we don't tell them?

> Our calling compels us to go forward preaching and teaching the Gospel.

The role of an ambassador in today's society is to speak on behalf of their government, represent their government, and assist their citizens. That's what God has called RevivalMakers to do.

Speak on behalf of God to the world.

Represent true Christianity to the world.

Love your brother and sisters.

There are many ways for RevivalMakers to fulfill their role as an ambassador within their local community.

As a father of five children, one specific area that has been heavy on my heart is that of our nation's schools. There is a very urgent need for prayer warriors to rise up and pray for our school systems again. It was once a common thing for churches to pray and even "prayer walk/march" around the schools in their communities. More than ever our children are in danger from school shootings and other threats taking place. This is a demonic phenomenon of this present age. It does not matter whether you live in a metropolitan or rural area, the threat is always there. We need to adopt our schools in prayer and ask the Lord to dispatch an army of angels to protect our children as they come and go as well as while they're learning.

> How will our children know what we stand for and why, if we don't tell them?

The threat of violence as a whole in society makes it seem like we're living in the old wild west.

While politicians debate gun control and defunding law enforcement, we as ambassadors of Christ fight this battle another way. Not only should we pray for law enforcement but we can assist them by adopting our communities in prayer. We know that the battles being waged on the earth are spiritual, not carnal. Knowing that the weapons of our warfare are not carnal, we can cover our communities in prayer. Our churches are filled with men and women who desire to enter ministry. We can equip these believers and train them in the gifts of the Spirit and set them loose on the streets of our city in the spirit of Luke 10, that they may go spreading the Gospel, praying for the sick, and binding the works of satan. This could arguably become the most important ministry within our local churches. We would be putting the power of God that lives on the inside of us to good use. What demon army could withstand that kind of holy army?

> I expect miracles. I expect healing. I expect revival.

Everywhere I go, I see tents set up to sell everything from cheap steaks to rugs, fireworks, and everything in between, but where are the prayer tents? RevivalMakers can set up tents in their community offering to pray with people. God can use you in that tent! If you've heard me preach before, you know I tell everyone that God is the original tent revivalist! God loves tents and tabernacles. It was His original idea for how to visit His people.

The fact is that our holy anger and frustration cannot simply manifest in our social media postings. We must take action—the kind where results can be measured. This goes back to a previous chapter on the necessity of the baptism of the Holy Ghost. Once God fills you, you are "endued with power." That power is not simply to speak in tongues in a church setting. The power is to be witnesses and evangelists. What better way than to go into our communities and, when the opportunity arises, be ready to spring into action?

While some may still yet find it controversial or too far-fetched of an idea, it is past time that more Spirit-filled believers run for office as well as occupy seats on our PTAs, educational boards, and any other board/committee that we can join. We cannot influence if we do not participate. We must be at the table to bring change! God will give you insight others won't have. God will give *you* the next "big idea" so that His name is glorified through you.

In a certain season of my life I spent about one day a week in Washington, DC, and absolutely loved it. It's a city that, like New York, never sleeps. There is always something happening somewhere;

you never know who you will see or what could be happening. One thing that always stood out to me and captured my attention was the foreign delegates. They were in DC, representing their nation of origin. You could pick their cars out from the rest because their license plates were different. They were here but identifying with somewhere else.

RevivalMakers, if you could see what the spirit world sees, you'd see the same. When principalities see you, they know you're different because you carry a different identifying mark—the name of *Jesus*. That name and the applied blood of the Lamb of God cause you to stand out. Spirits recognize you live here but you're not from here—you are ambassadors of another world/kingdom, and of its government there shall be no end.

ed separately from one another.

THE RIVER OF REVIVAL

If you're in a Spirit-filled church there's a good chance you've heard about "streams," pertaining to spiritual ancestry. Some come from the Pentecostal stream or charismatic stream, others from the word of faith, others from the apostolic, and so on and so forth. Each stream carries truth that the entire body needs, but for the most part these streams have functioned separately from one another. Every now and then there is crossover from one to the other, but we have yet to see a full unity of the streams.

> We have yet to see a full unity of the streams.

Each stream of revival has passed through a controversy at some point. For the sake of a word picture, let's call it a "pollution." What I have observed is that rather than clean up the pollution or deal with error when it creeps in, the body at large will cap off the stream completely. This is grievous error because each stream comes from the throne room of God with revelation we need.

Without the stream of Pentecost the church has no power. Without the charismatic stream the church has no giftings. Without the word of faith the church has no authority. Without the stream of joy the church loses its attractiveness. Without prosperity the church cannot take dominion.

> Each stream comes from the throne room of God with revelation we need.

So many have been exposed to a measure of truth—one stream of revival, one manifestation of the Holy Spirit—yet are hungry for more. I contend the church needs every stream, every measure of truth and the fullness of the Holy Spirit's power and demonstration. Why settle when you can have it all?

Ecology teaches that a stream is a flow of water that follows a temporary path. It cannot survive forever alone; therefore, it'll combine with other tributaries and form a river system, and a river is a permanent flow down a permanent path.

That's what I'm seeking! I'm after the river of revival where the fullness of the move of God is found. In the unity of the streams of the spirit, rather than dividing into streams, we feed the river of revival with each stream of truth. Thus, the church operates in full power and dominion. I believe that river flowed in the first-century church. The original apostles and believers were not broken into streams but were united. Even though there was a diversity of giftings (see 1 Cor. 12), they were unified in revival.

When measuring the strength of a stream or river, ecologists will study what is called "streamflow." Streamflow measures the velocity of a river, as well as the amount of water that is flowing through it. Those things affect the water quality, therefore impacting the communities, animals, and human lives. The streamflow affects everything living in the river and depending on the river. I don't want a dip of power, a drizzle of prosperity, or a dribble of authority. I don't need a trickle of joy and a teaspoon of anointing. I want the fullness of the river of revival. A streamflow that, when measured by the Word, shows a river *full* of

> I don't need a trickle of joy and a teaspoon of anointing. I want the fullness of the river of revival.

prosperity and power, *full* of joy and authority, *full* of every benefit that comes from the Holy Spirit.

RevivalMakers, this river of revival that flows from the very mountain of God can be accessed by every believer willing to find it. It's found in hungry pursuit of Him. It's found by those who aren't satisfied with just one stream but are pursuing the fullness of Him.

About Tony Suarez

Tony Suarez is the founder of RevivalMakers, a Spirit-filled evangelistic ministry that travels from church to church as well as hosts events, tent revivals, healing services, and crusades around the world. A third-generation Pentecostal preacher, Tony's greatest passion in life is preaching and teaching about Jesus and watching God save and heal. He is a regular host and guest on TBN and the Victory Channel. His preaching ministry and program RevivalMakers can be found daily on various Christian outlets. In addition to his ministry work, Tony serves as the Chief Operating Officer of the National Hispanic Christian Leadership Conference (NHCLC), the nation's largest Hispanic Christian organization, serving more than 40,000 congregations in the United States as well as thousands of churches abroad. Through his role as COO, Pastor Tony regularly meets with members of Congress, the White House, and speaks at events to advance the cause of righteousness, life, and religious liberty. Tony and his wife Jina, along with their five children, reside in Tennessee.

YOUR

Prophetic

COMMUNITY

Are you passionate about hearing God's voice, walking with Jesus, and experiencing the power of the Holy Spirit?

Destiny Image is a community of believers with a passion for equipping and encouraging you to live the prophetic, supernatural life you were created for!

We offer a fresh helping of practical articles, dynamic podcasts, and powerful videos from respected, Spirit-empowered, Christian leaders to fuel the holy fire within you.

Sign up now to get awesome content delivered to your inbox
destinyimage.com/sign-up

 Destiny Image

9 780768 462258